EYEWITNESS
WEATHER

19th-century
aneroid barometer

Statue of an
Aztec sun god

Shut pine
cone signals
wet weather

Open pine
cone signals
dry weather

Fitzroy
barometer

REVISED EDITION

DK LONDON
Senior Editor Carron Brown
Project Editor Vicky Richards
Senior Art Editor Lynne Moulding
Art Editor Chrissy Barnard
US Editor Jennette ElNaggar
US Executive Editor Lori Cates Hand
Managing Editor Francesca Baines
Managing Art Editor Philip Letsu
Production Editor Kavita Varma
Production Controller Sian Cheung
Senior Jackets Designer Surabhi Wadhwa-Gandhi
Jacket Design Development Manager Sophia MTT
Publisher Andrew Macintyre
Associate Publishing Director Liz Wheeler
Art Director Karen Self
Publishing Director Jonathan Metcalf

Consultant Sam Hardy

DK DELHI
Senior Editor Shatarupa Chaudhuri
Senior Art Editor Vikas Chauhan
Project Art Editor Mansi Agrawal
Editor Sai Prasanna
Picture Researcher Vishal Ghavri
Managing Editor Kingshuk Ghoshal
Managing Art Editor Govind Mittal
DTP Designers Pawan Kumar, Rakesh Kumar,
Nityanand Kumar
Jacket Designer Juhi Sheth

FIRST EDITION
Project Editors John Farndon, Marion Dent
Art Editor Alison Anholt-White
Senior Editor Helen Parker
Senior Art Editors Jacquie Gulliver, Julia Harris
Production Louise Barratt **Picture Researcher** Diana Morris
Special Photography Karl Shone, Keith Percival
Editorial Consultant Jim Sharp

This Eyewitness ® Book has been conceived by
Dorling Kindersley Limited and Editions Gallimard

This American Edition, 2022
First American Edition, 1992
Published in the United States by DK Publishing
1450 Broadway, Suite 801, New York, NY 10018

Copyright © 1991, 2002, 2007, 2016, 2022
Dorling Kindersley Limited
DK, a Division of Penguin Random House LLC
22 23 24 25 26 10 9 8 7 6 5 4 3 2 1
001-327183-May/2022

A catalog record for this book is available
from the Library of Congress.
ISBN 978-0-7440-5230-5 (Paperback)
ISBN 978-0-7440-5231-2 (ALB)

Printed and bound in China

For the curious
www.dk.com

MIX
Paper from
responsible sources
FSC™ C018179

This book was made with Forest Stewardship Council™ certified
paper—one small step in DK's commitment to a sustainable future.
For more information go to www.dk.com/our-green-pledge

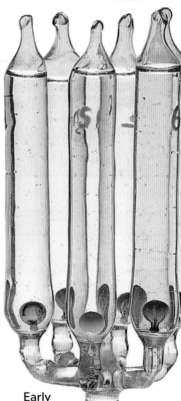

Early
Florentine
glass
thermometer

EYEWITNESS
WEATHER

Weather on the plains

Model of a
cold front

Snow
crystal

Hot-air balloon

Weathercock

Mountain weather

Model of mountain
weather patterns

Early Florentine
mercury barometer
and thermometer

Hygrometer

Contents

Orrery from the 18th century showing the movement of the planet and the seasons

The restless **air**

Our planet is surrounded by a blanket of gases called the atmosphere. These gases protect us from the intense heat of the sun in the day and the freezing temperatures of night. The very lowest 6 miles (10 km) of the atmosphere—the air in which we live and breathe—is known as the troposphere. This layer of air is forever on the move, boiling and bubbling in the sun's heat. It is the constant swirling of the troposphere that gives us our weather, from the warm, still days of summer to the wildest storms of winter.

Taking the air
In the 19th century, scientists in hot-air balloons found that the air got colder the higher they went. Uncrewed balloons later proved that air gets colder only up to a certain point—the tropopause, or the top of the troposphere.

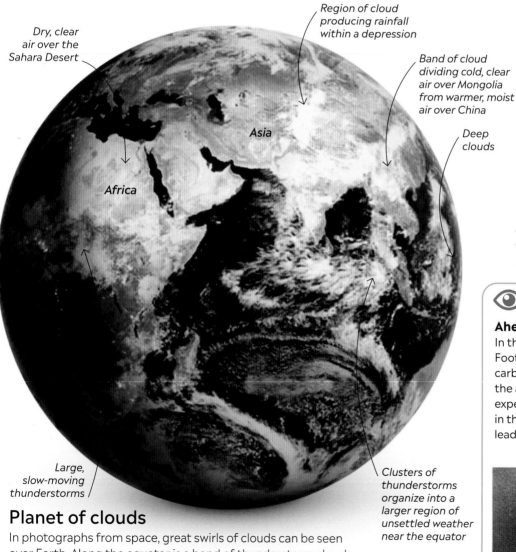

Dry, clear air over the Sahara Desert

Region of cloud producing rainfall within a depression

Band of cloud dividing cold, clear air over Mongolia from warmer, moist air over China

Deep clouds

Asia

Africa

Large, slow-moving thunderstorms

Clusters of thunderstorms organize into a larger region of unsettled weather near the equator

Planet of clouds
In photographs from space, great swirls of clouds can be seen over Earth. Along the equator is a band of thunderstorm clouds, formed by the intense heat of the sun stirring up rising currents of air. These carry moisture from the ocean so high into the air that it cools and turns into water droplets, forming clouds.

What is air?
In the 1780s, French chemist Antoine Lavoisier discovered that air contained three main gases: oxygen, nitrogen, and carbon dioxide.

 EYEWITNESS

Ahead of her time
In the 1850s, American scientist Eunice Foote (1819–1888) discovered that carbon dioxide (CO_2) absorbs heat in the atmosphere, using a laboratory experiment. She suggested that a rise in the CO_2 level in the atmosphere leads to an increase in temperature.

World of weather

Some weather systems stretch right around the world. Tropical storms and hurricanes spin across the Atlantic and Pacific oceans, visible as dense masses of clouds. Between the poles and the tropics, larger spiral-shaped depressions move from west to east. These develop because the turning of the Earth spins the winds flowing between the poles.

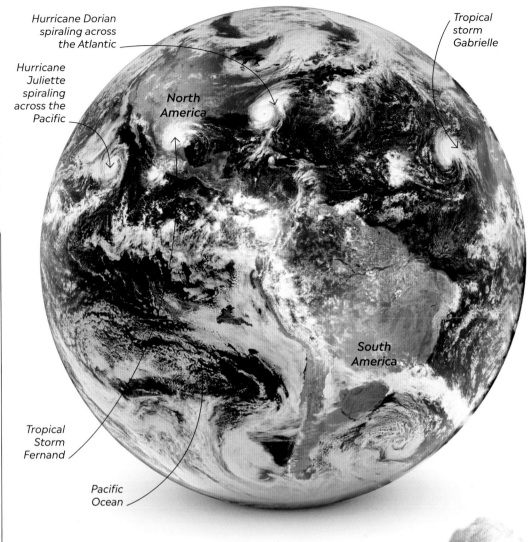

Hurricane Dorian spiraling across the Atlantic

Tropical storm Gabrielle

Hurricane Juliette spiraling across the Pacific

North America

South America

Tropical Storm Fernand

Pacific Ocean

HOT AND COLD AIR

The air in the atmosphere gets hotter or colder depending on the layer. In the troposphere, the temperature drops steadily as you climb. Right up in the thermosphere, however, temperatures can rise to 3,600°F (2,000°C).

Height in miles

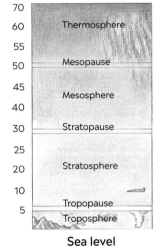

Height	Layer
70	
60	Thermosphere
55	
50	Mesopause
45	Mesosphere
40	
30	Stratopause
25	
20	Stratosphere
10	
5	Tropopause
	Troposphere

Sea level

Above the weather

Weather occurs only in the troposphere because this layer contains the most moisture—in the form of an invisible gas called water vapor. Flying through clouds in the troposphere can be bumpy, so pilots often fly above the clouds, in the stratosphere, where the air is still and clear.

Glorious morning

The petals of morning glory open and shut in response to the weather. These wide-open blooms indicate fine weather.

Natural signs

Sailors, farmers, and others whose livelihood depends on the weather learned long ago that the natural world can provide useful clues about the weather to come. Many of these natural signs are based on superstition. But tiny variations in the air, which we cannot feel, often affect plants and animals. A change in their appearance or behavior may be a sign of a change in the weather.

Sun day opening

The scarlet pimpernel has long been used to predict the weather. Its tiny flowers open wide in sunny weather but close up tightly when rain is in the air.

Weather weed

In fine weather, seaweed shrivels and becomes dry. If rain threatens, the weed swells and feels damp.

Sunset

Sunrise

Seeing red

According to tradition, a red sunset means that fine weather will follow, while a red sunrise means that storms are on the way.

Fleeing danger

Scientists say some birds can sense bad weather, such as storms, approaching. For example, warblers fly away from the path of the storm, while others, like pelicans (right), may hide behind barrier islands.

Wet   Dry

Weather cones

A pine cone is one of the most reliable natural weather predictors. In dry weather, the scales on the cone shrivel up and open out. When rain is on the way, the scales shut tightly.

Cricket forecast

Crickets are sensitive to changes in the weather, chirping louder and louder as the temperature rises. The chirping sound is made by their hind legs rubbing against their hard front wings.

Great green bush cricket

Oak   Ash

Soak or splash?

An old English saying states: *If the oak flowers before the ash, we shall have a splash* (meaning only light rain for the next month or so). *If the ash flowers before the oak, we shall have a soak* (meaning very wet weather). However, there is no evidence to support this prediction.

Groundhog Day

In the US, February 2 is Groundhog Day. It is said that if a groundhog's shadow appears at noon, it will be cold for the next six weeks.

Telling tail

Some country folk expect a severe winter if squirrels have very bushy tails or gather big stores of nuts in the fall.

Flowering horse chestnut tree

Spring is here

The blooming of white flowers on the horse chestnut tree is said to herald the end of winter. These flowers will only appear once the weather is mild enough.

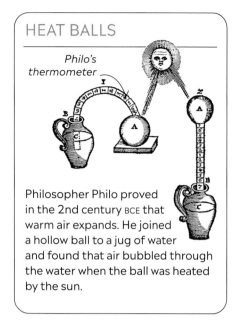

Philo's thermometer

Philosopher Philo proved in the 2nd century BCE that warm air expands. He joined a hollow ball to a jug of water and found that air bubbled through the water when the ball was heated by the sun.

The science of weather

Weather and the atmosphere have fascinated scientists for centuries. Aristotle, the Greek philosopher, studied the atmosphere and coined the word "meteorology"—the science of weather. In 17th-century Italy, scientists developed the first instruments to measure changes in the atmosphere. In around 1600, Italian physicist Galileo Galilei created the first thermometer. The first barometer for measuring air pressure was developed 40 years later by his assistant Torricelli. The first really successful thermometer was made by German physicist Daniel Fahrenheit in about 1709.

Wet or dry

This 18th-century hygrometer was designed to measure the moisture content of the air. A pile of soft paper discs are placed on one arm. If the air is dry, the discs weigh less. If the air is damp, they absorb water and weigh more, pulling the pointer up.

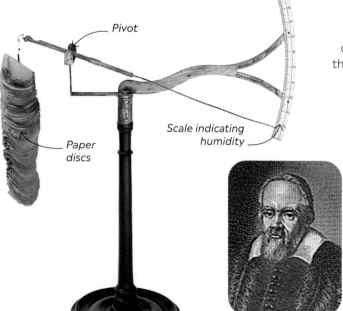

Pivot

Scale indicating humidity

Paper discs

Icy water

This replica of an early hygrometer (right) has a hollow core that can be filled with ice. Moisture in the air cools and condenses (turns into water droplets) on the outside then runs down into a measuring flask. The amount of water collected in the flask indicates the moisture content of the air.

Flask for collecting water

Paper strip

Galileo

Galileo believed that air had weight, or pressure, and asked his assistant Torricelli to carry out experiments that would prove his theories.

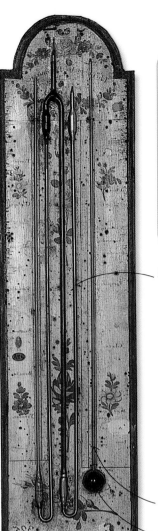

Barometer

First barometer

Evangelista Torricelli (1608-1647) made the first barometer in 1644 and proved the existence of air pressure—the force of air pressing down on a surface. He showed that changes in the atmospheric pressure led to changes in the mercury level in his barometer.

Early weather

The Italian script on this early barometer describes various different types of weather conditions.

Italian script

Needle indicating air pressure

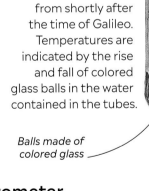

Weather academy

This painting shows a group of Italian scientists in 1657. Using a thermometer, a mirror, and a bucket of ice, they are trying to find out if cold, like heat, can be reflected. It cannot.

Thermometer

Mercury reservoir

Mercury tube

This 18th-century mercury barometer and thermometer was designed to measure air pressure. When the air pressure is high, it weighs heavily on the liquid mercury in the glass tube at the base, and pushes the mercury up the tube. When air pressure is low, the level of mercury drops.

Surface of water in tube

Crown glass

This ornate glass thermometer dates from shortly after the time of Galileo. Temperatures are indicated by the rise and fall of colored glass balls in the water contained in the tubes.

Balls made of colored glass

Dial hygrometer

The needle of this early hygrometer is moved by a paper strip that shrinks or stretches in response to the dampness of the air.

Round dial

Watching the weather

Meteorologists (weather scientists) gather information about the weather from a wide range of sources. A global network of weather stations constantly monitors conditions on land and at sea. Weather balloons and research aircraft are sent high into the atmosphere, while out in space, satellites circle the Earth, beaming back pictures of cloud and temperature patterns.

Air sampler

"Blister" on fuselage houses monitoring equipment

Nose of plane is studded with sensors

Plane carries a crew of three and up to 18 scientists

Weather watcher

There are two types of weather satellites. Geostationary satellites stay fixed in the same spot and provide an almost complete picture of the globe (except for the two poles) every half hour. Polar-orbiting satellites circle the Earth from pole to pole. They provide a changing, more detailed weather picture from closer to Earth's surface.

Thermometers in ventilated white surround

Wind vane for measuring wind direction

Anemometer for measuring wind speed

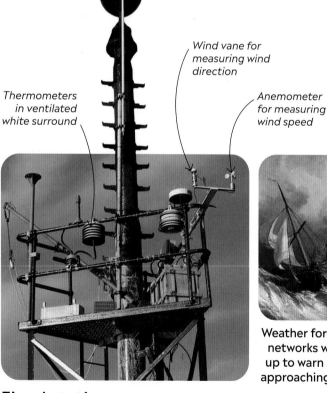

Weather forecasting networks were set up to warn ships of approaching storms.

Solar panel to power navigation light

Transmitter aerial

Transmitter gives buoy position to orbiting satellite

Sea watch

Drifting weather buoys are used to provide information about conditions at sea. The buoys float in the ocean currents and send back data via satellites. The satellites can pinpoint where the buoy is to within 1 mile (2 km).

Fixed station

The World Meteorological Organization has a network of about 11,000 permanent weather stations around the world. Every three hours, weather reports are sent to forecasting centers in individual countries so they can create their own weather forecasts.

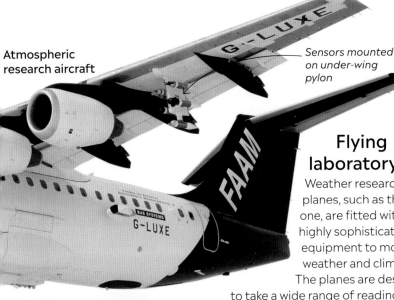

Atmospheric research aircraft

Sensors mounted on under-wing pylon

G-LUXE

FAAM

G-LUXE

Flying laboratory

Weather research planes, such as this one, are fitted with highly sophisticated equipment to monitor weather and climate. The planes are designed to take a wide range of readings at different levels in the atmosphere. Some can even fly right into the eye of a hurricane to get detailed information on wind speed, air pressure, temperature, and humidity.

Onboard scientist checking data

Measuring rainfall intensity
Joanne Simpson (1923–2010) was the first female US meteorologist with a doctorate degree. She researched tropical cyclones and helped develop the Tropical Rainfall Measuring Mission (TRMM) satellite. The rainfall intensity measurements from this satellite have notably improved tropical cyclone forecasting.

Madagascar seen from a NASA satellite

High view

Satellite images help monitor the weather. Satellites use both infrared and microwave radiation to measure temperature. Clouds are measured using reflected sunlight and winds by tracking the motion of clouds.

Sky probe

Twice a day, nearly a thousand weather balloons filled with helium gas are launched into the atmosphere across the world. Attached to each balloon is a package of instruments called a radiosonde. These instruments take humidity, temperature, and pressure readings, and radio the results back to Earth.

Balloon is tracked either by radar or with survey equipment

Tube for filling balloon with helium gas

EYEWITNESS

Joseph Henry (1797–1878)
In 1848, Joseph Henry set up a system to obtain up-to-date weather reports from across the US. By 1849, more than 200 people were sending measurements back to Mr. Henry at the Smithsonian Institute in Washington. The data was used to provide daily weather reports for the *Washington Evening Post*.

Forecasting

Every minute, weather observations taken by weather stations, ships, satellites, balloons, and radar all around the world are fed into powerful supercomputers, able to carry out millions of calculations each second. Meteorologists use this information to make short-range weather forecasts for the next 24 hours and draw up a weather map, or "synoptic chart," showing air pressure, temperature, wind, cloud cover, and humidity (moisture in the air). They can also make fairly accurate long-range forecasts for up to a week.

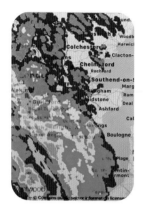

Physicist Jean de Borda linked changes in air pressure to wind speed.

Rain scan

Radar signals reflect rain, hail, and snow. The intensity of the reflection shows how heavily rain is falling. Meteorologists use this data to create a map of rainfall intensity, as above.

Blue sky

Fair weather, with blue sky and light cloud, is often linked to high-pressure zones, or "anticyclones."

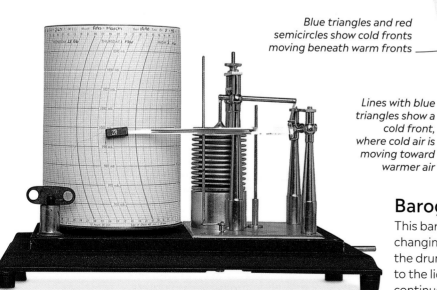

Blue triangles and red semicircles show cold fronts moving beneath warm fronts

Lines with blue triangles show a cold front, where cold air is moving toward warmer air

Barograph

This barograph (left) makes a continuous record of changing air pressure. As the air pressure changes, the drum expands and contracts. A pen attached to the lid of the drum draws the ups and downs continuously on a rotating sheet of graph paper.

Storm by satellite

The cold front and depression, marked on the synoptic chart (below), are clearly revealed by the whirl of clouds in this satellite photograph (left).

Dull days

Wet and stormy weather is often associated with fronts and low-pressure zones, or depressions.

Closely spaced isobars indicate strong wind

Low, or depression

Charting the weather

The most obvious features on any weather map, or synoptic chart, are the long, curved lines called isobars. These lines link points of equal air pressure and are usually measured in millibars (mb). The inside circles linked by low-pressure isobars are depressions, where the air is rising. These frequently bring wind, clouds, and rain. The inside circles linked by high-pressure isobars are highs, where air is sinking. These usually bring dry, settled weather.

Weather station, with observations for wind, cloud cover, and other factors (see key)

Isobar joining points of equal air pressure

Lines with red semicircles show a warm front, where warm air is pushing over cold air

Richardson

In the 1920s, Lewis Richardson devised "numeric weather predictions." He believed that the key to weather forecasting was to observe weather conditions at evenly spaced points across the world at the same time. He tried with this purpose-built calculator, but the calculations were too huge. Numeric forecasting has only become possible with the development of supercomputers.

Temperature: 45°F (7°C)

Current weather: heavy rain

Visibility: 1.5 miles (2.5 km)

Dew point: 43°F (6°C)

Stratus cloud

Cloud cover complete

Air pressure: 1,018 mb

Moderate, north-easterly wind

Pressure fallen by 2.7 mb in last 3 hours

Rain in past hour

Cloud base height (1,310 ft/400 m)

07   180

25   27

06

8/12

Key to symbols and numbers

The sun

Solar storms

Here we see gigantic explosions, called solar flares and storms erupting at the sun's surface. These storms can impact the entire solar system, including Earth and its magnetosphere.

Weather happens because the sun's heat keeps the atmosphere in constant motion. But the sun's power to heat the air varies—across the world, through the day, and through the year. All these variations depend on the sun's height in the sky. When the sun is high in the sky, its rays strike the ground directly, giving maximum heat. When it is low, the rays strike the ground at an angle, spreading the heat over a wider area. The atmosphere absorbs much of the sun's heat, but Earth stays warm because greenhouse gases trap the heat in the air.

Hot spots

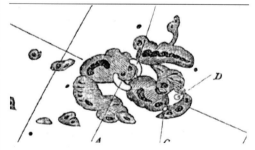

Deserts occur wherever the air is very dry so few clouds can form. They can be hot, such as the Sahara, or cold, such as the Gobi in central Asia.

Polar cold

Vast areas of the Arctic and Antarctic are covered in a permanent sheet of ice.

Daily rhythms

The shadow cast by the needle, or "gnomon," of a sundial shifts as the sun moves through the sky from sunrise to sunset, indicating the time of day.

Gnomon

18th-century brass sundial

CARRINGTON EVENT

In 1859, astronomer Richard Carrington observed the sun using a simple telescope. As he sketched dark areas called sunspots (above), two blinding spots of light erupted from the sun, causing him to look away from the screen. Named the Carrington Event, the solar flares that he had observed were part of the largest space weather event ever recorded.

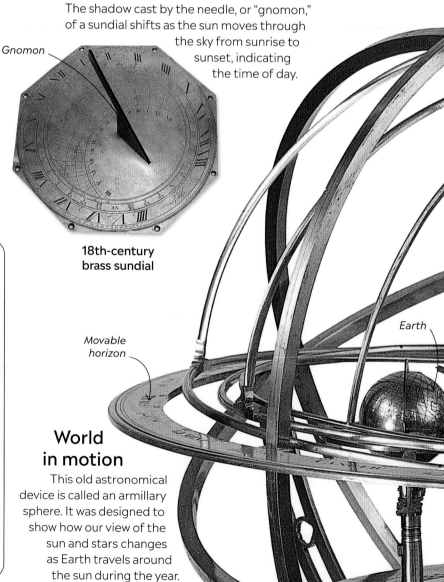

Movable horizon

Earth

World in motion

This old astronomical device is called an armillary sphere. It was designed to show how our view of the sun and stars changes as Earth travels around the sun during the year.

Seasoned weather

In the tropics, there are often just two seasons in the year, one wet and one dry. In hot deserts, there are no real seasons, as the weather changes little through the year. But in the temperate zones, the weather passes through four distinct phases during the year: spring, summer, fall, and winter.

14th-century illustration of summer

THE WORLD'S CLIMATES

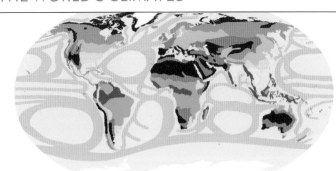

As the Earth is round, the sun's rays strike different parts at different angles, creating distinct climate zones. Climate is the average weather of a particular place over a period of time. The hottest places are the tropics along the equator, where the sun is almost overhead at noon. The coldest places are the poles, where the sun's rays are spread over a wide area. In between these extremes lie the temperate zones.

- Desert
- Semi-desert
- Temperate
- Tundra
- Monsoon
- Subarctic
- Subtropical
- Polar
- Mediterranean

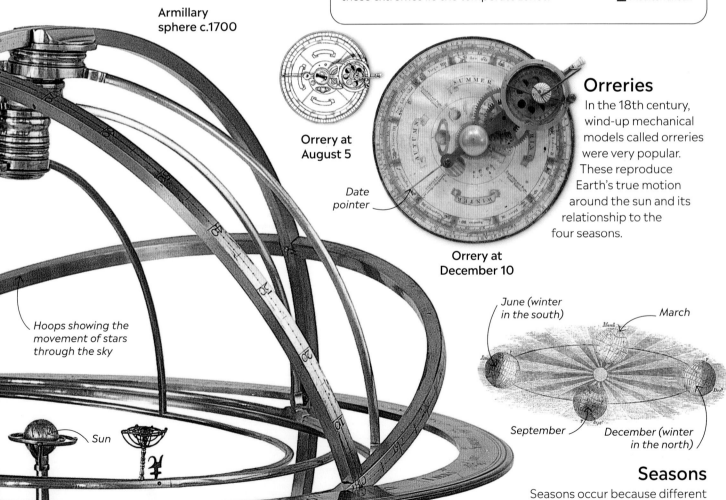

Armillary sphere c.1700

Orrery at August 5

Date pointer

Orreries

In the 18th century, wind-up mechanical models called orreries were very popular. These reproduce Earth's true motion around the sun and its relationship to the four seasons.

Orrery at December 10

Hoops showing the movement of stars through the sky

Sun

June (winter in the south)

March

September

December (winter in the north)

Seasons

Seasons occur because different parts of Earth are tilted toward the sun during the year. When parts of Earth are tilted away from the sun, the days are short, bringing winter. When parts of Earth tilt toward the sun, the days are long, bringing summer. Between these two extremes lie spring and fall.

A sunny day

Over much of the world, sunny weather and clear skies are common, especially in summer. Clouds form only when there is enough moisture in the air. Dry, sunny weather is often associated with high pressure, where air in the atmosphere sinks slowly, compressing (squashing) the air below and preventing clouds from forming. In summer, high pressure can last for days, bringing long spells of warm, dry weather.

The annual average temperature of Dallol in Ethiopia is 94°F (34.4°C).

Sun god

So important was reliable sunshine in ancient times—not only for heat and light but also for ripening crops—that many early civilizations worshipped the sun. The Aztecs of Mexico, in particular, built vast temples to their sun god Tonatiuh.

Plants need sunlight to make their food in leaves.

Growing light

Green plants need plenty of sunshine, as all their energy for growth comes directly from the sun.

Solar cell panel on a rooftop

Solar power

Most of our energy comes from the sun. Light-sensitive crystals in solar cells enable us to convert light energy from the sun into electricity.

Burning record

Meteorologists can record hours of sunshine on a device called a Campbell-Stokes sunshine recorder (right). A glass ball focuses the sun's rays onto a strip of card so that they burn the card. As the sun moves round during the day, so do the scorch marks on the paper, giving a complete record of the day's sunshine.

Image of the sun reflected in glass

Burn marks on card

Wisps of high cirrus clouds, made entirely of ice. These may be traces of a vanished storm cloud, since ice turns into water vapor more slowly than water. But they could signal the arrival of a warm front.

Blue sky

In summer, sunny days tend to be hot, as there is little cloud to block out the sun's rays. But without clouds to trap the heat rising from the ground, temperatures can often drop rapidly after sunset. Clear, blue skies may look uninteresting at first sight, but there is often plenty going on, especially when the atmosphere is humid or dusty.

The sunniest place on Earth is the city of Yuma, Arizona, which receives more than 4,000 hours of sunshine each year.

1020
1028
HIGH

Trails of water vapor left by jet planes, especially in cold, moist air. Made of ice, these trails of vapor, called contrails, form when the hot gases that shoot out behind a plane hit cool air and rise rapidly. As they rise, they expand and freeze almost immediately.

Small, short-lived, fluffy cumulus clouds may be formed here and there by rising warm air currents.

Frost and ice

Temperatures are rarely high in winter, and at night, heat in the ground can flow away quickly. On a clear, dry winter night, temperatures near the ground can fall so low that water vapor in the air freezes, forming white crystals called frost. Frosts are rare in the tropics but are almost continuous toward the poles. In the midlatitudes, frosts occur more often inland than near the coast, where the sea tends to keep its heat longer.

Frosty hands

The fictional "Jack Frost" is said to leave icy finger marks on window panes.

Icy coating

When the conditions are cold enough, moisture from the air freezes, leaving surfaces coated with a thin layer of ice crystals. In spring and fall, frosts can occur when heat rises from the ground on clear nights. In midwinter, though, a chill polar wind may be enough to bring frost.

Thick coating of rime, a white ice formed when an icy wind blows over leaves, branches, and other surfaces. Temperatures usually have to be lower for rime than for hoar frost.

Hoar frost coats freezing cold surfaces, such as soil and metal, with ice crystals.

Icing up

High in the atmosphere, air temperatures are always below freezing, and the wings of airplanes can easily become coated with ice.

Hoar thorns

When water vapor touches a very cold surface, it can freeze instantly, leaving spiky needles of "hoar frost." The frost tends to occur when the temperature is around 32°F (0°C), but the air must be moist to create the ice crystals.

Cold frame

In severe weather, delicate "fern frost" patterns may appear on windows. Drops of moisture called dew form on the cold glass. As they freeze, they turn into ice crystals, forming beautiful patterns.

Frozen arch

Sometimes vast chunks of ice, or icebergs, break off polar glaciers and float out to sea. Icebergs float because water becomes less dense when it freezes, but most of their bulk lies below the water.

Even though there is a mist near the ground, the sky above is clear, allowing heat to escape during the night.

Frost is white because the crystals contain air.

HIGH

LOW

The low temperatures near the ground that bring frost can also create fog. The moisture condenses in the cold air and hangs there, because there is little wind to disperse it. If the fog coats surfaces with ice, it is called freezing fog.

Ice house

Most icicles form when drips of melting snow freeze. This industrial warehouse in Chicago got its remarkable coat of ice when firemen sprayed water on it to put out a fire in harsh winter conditions.

Market on ice

In the early 1800s, frosts could be so hard that even the Thames River in London froze solid. The last "frost fair" held on the ice was in 1814.

Wet **air**

Even on the sunniest days, the horizon often shimmers in a haze. Some haze is dust and pollution, but most is simply moisture in the air. Like a dry sponge, the air soaks up water that is constantly rising up from Earth's surface. Most of the moisture in the air is in the form of an invisible gas called water vapor. If water vapor cools enough in the air, it turns into droplets of water in a process called condensation. Clouds, mist, and haze are all formed from these tiny droplets.

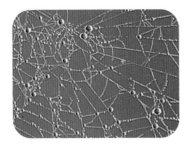

Dew drops

Water vapor condenses as air cools. The cooler the air, the less water vapor it can hold. Once air reaches the limit of moisture it can hold, the water vapor condenses into droplets. This is called the dew point.

Scale shows humidity

Hair hygrometer

Human hair

Wet hair

Humidity (the moisture content of the air) can be measured using an instrument called a hair hygrometer (above). It contains a piece of human hair that stretches in moist air and shrinks in dry air.

When the water level in the spout is high, pressure is low and storms can be expected

Closed glass bulb

When working, the level of water in the weather glass would have been much higher

Storm glass

Like mercury in a barometer, water levels can be used to monitor air pressure. Though not accurate, "weather glasses" like this (above) were cheaper to make than mercury barometers.

Weather house

Weather houses like the one shown here are actually hair hygrometers. If the air is moist, a hair inside the house stretches and lets the man out. If the air is dry, the hair shrinks, pulling the man in and letting the woman out.

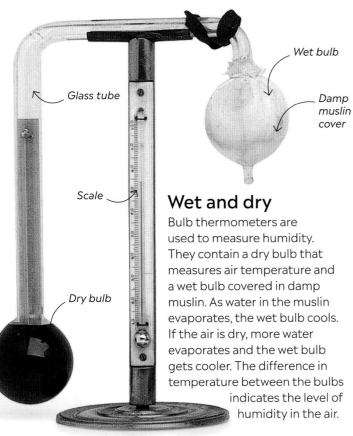

Glass tube

Wet bulb

Damp muslin cover

Scale

Dry bulb

Wet and dry

Bulb thermometers are used to measure humidity. They contain a dry bulb that measures air temperature and a wet bulb covered in damp muslin. As water in the muslin evaporates, the wet bulb cools. If the air is dry, more water evaporates and the wet bulb gets cooler. The difference in temperature between the bulbs indicates the level of humidity in the air.

Antique version of a bulb thermometer

Small measures

Modern hygrometers measure humidity by calculating the ability of a sample of air to store electric charge. These instruments are more durable than older models, which used human hair to measure humidity.

Mountain mist

In mountain areas, mist will often gather in the valleys in the morning because cold air flows downhill in the night and settles there.

Damp work

Silkworm caterpillars making silk fiber need warmth and moisture. If the air is not damp enough, the caterpillars will not spin the thread as efficiently.

Raindrops

Unless a raindrop is big to start with, a phenomenon known as surface tension will hold it on to a pane of glass until another drop falls in the same place. This breaks the tension, and the drops run down the pane together. In the same way, tiny droplets of water in a cloud will only start to fall as rain when they are large and heavy enough.

Raindrop just large enough to overcome tension

Small raindrops held on glass by surface tension

Large drop gathers others in its path

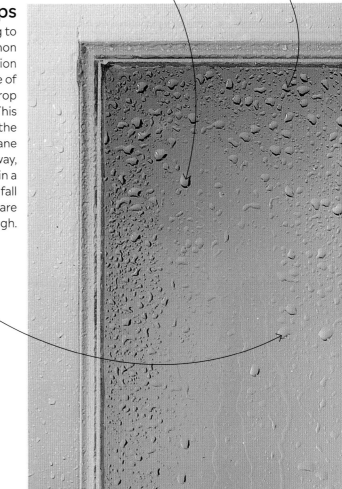

Water vision

Even on clear days, there is often a slight haze in the air, making distant hills look soft and pale.

Thermals

Bubbles of warm air, called thermals, form over hot spots on the ground. The warm air drifts up and expands into the cooler air around it. As the air rises, it cools down, until at a certain height—the condensation level—it is so cool that the moisture it contains condenses into water droplets.

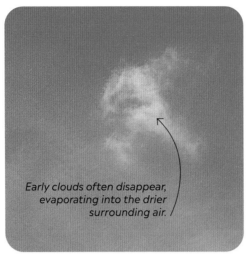

Early clouds often disappear, evaporating into the drier surrounding air.

1. Small beginnings
It takes some time for the sun to heat the ground, so the first clouds are very small.

In the morning, when the thermals are weak, small, individual clouds form, with clear sky between them.

2. New bubbles
Sometimes, the clouds formed by bubbles of warm air will drift away in the wind, and others will take their place, creating lines of clouds for many miles.

Birth of a cloud

On a fine day, you may see fleecy, "cotton ball" clouds constantly changing in shape and size. New clouds keep appearing, while others shrink and vanish. These short-lived clouds are called cumulus, or "heap" clouds. They are formed when the sun heats a patch of ground, creating a bubble of warm, moist air. The bubble drifts upward, and as it rises, it cools and condenses to form a cloud. Bubbles like these rarely last for more than 20 minutes. Often, several bubbles drift up in the same place. If this happens, the clouds may build up so much that a rain shower occurs. Occasionally, cumulus clouds billow high into the atmosphere and turn into huge thunderclouds, resulting in a terrific downpour.

Hot air

As air heats up, it becomes lighter than the cooler air around it and starts to rise. The Montgolfier brothers used this principle when they filled a balloon with hot air to make the first-ever manned flight over Paris, in 1783.

Steam clouds

Steam from an engine's funnel forms in much the same way as a cloud. As hot, moist air leaves the funnel, it expands and cools, until it gets so cold that it condenses into water droplets, forming steam.

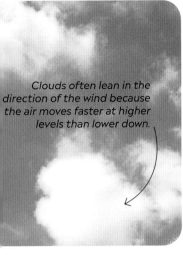

Clouds often lean in the direction of the wind because the air moves faster at higher levels than lower down.

Clouds appear brilliantly white in sunshine because the tiny water droplets reflect light extremely well.

A thick cloud has a very dark base because no sunlight passes through the cloud from above.

3. Building clouds

Clouds disappear only if the surrounding air is dry. They last longer as the day goes by, as the rising air brings in new moisture.

4. Up, up, and away

As the day heats up, more thermals drift upward. If one arrives close behind another, a single cloud is created.

5. High fliers

The movement of air inside cumulus clouds often becomes organized into "cells," with strong currents of air rising and falling quite close to each other. Pilots try to avoid flying through large cumulus clouds because these sudden updrafts and downdrafts of air can lead to a very bumpy ride.

Cumulus cloud forming from air released by chimneys

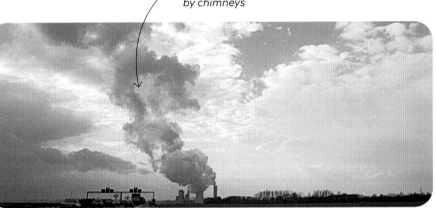

Artificial clouds

Not all clouds are natural ones. Inside power station cooling towers, the large quantities of cool water produce enormous volumes of very moist, slightly warm air, which often condenses immediately above the towers into low, "artificial" cumulus clouds.

Elk's breath

If the air is very cold, moisture in the elk's breath will condense into water droplets, which turn into tiny clouds.

A CLOUD FORMS

Clouds form when moist air is lifted high enough into the air to cool and condense (1). The sun heats a patch of ground, sending up bubbles of rising warm air (2). Fleecy cumulus clouds appear and disappear when these bubbles no longer form (3).

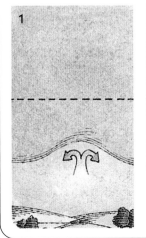

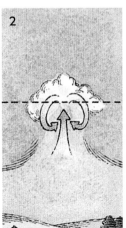

A cloudy
day

Lingering cloudy skies are usually associated with layered, or stratus, clouds that build up over a wide area when warm, moist air meets colder air. As this warm air rides slowly up over cold air, it steadily condenses as it cools, creating a vast blanket of cloud that can be several hundred yards thick and stretch for hundreds of miles.

Stratus cloud

Small cumulus clouds are unlikely to give much rain – although there might be light showers later in the day.

Three kinds of clouds

On some days, several types of clouds can be seen at different heights in the sky. In this picture (right), there are not only stratus and cumulus clouds but also a third type, called lenticular clouds. These lens-shaped clouds form near mountain ranges, where mountains disturb the airflow and create waves in the wind.

UPS AND DOWNS

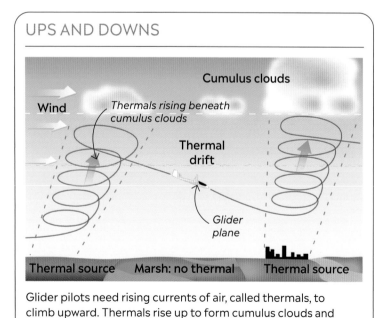

Cumulus clouds

Wind

Thermals rising beneath cumulus clouds

Thermal drift

Glider plane

Thermal source Marsh: no thermal Thermal source

Glider pilots need rising currents of air, called thermals, to climb upward. Thermals rise up to form cumulus clouds and are common over warm areas of land. However, they will not form over cooler bodies of water, such as lakes, so the gliders sink back down toward the ground. The same thing happens if thick layers of clouds cover the sky and cut off the warmth of the sunlight from the ground.

Cloud height

Today, meteorologists use ceilometers, devices that use a laser or a similar light source to measure the height of a cloud or cloud base. Cloud cover, however, is figured out visually, by estimating roughly what proportion of the sky is covered by the cloud directly overhead.

Altocumulus and altostratus clouds (the word "alto" refers to medium-height clouds)

The cloud cover is extensive, but there are still patches of blue sky visible.

Lenticular clouds stay in the same place until conditions change.

When there are several layers of humid air, lenticular clouds appear to be stacked on top of one another like a pile of plates.

Good visibility in the clear air beneath the clouds

Smooth or lumpy

The Beauty of the Heavens by Charles F. Blunt showed two main groups of clouds: cumulus (right), which are heaped clouds formed by the rise of individual bubbles of air, and cirrostratus (left), where whole layers of air are forced to rise, forming widespread sheets of clouds.

Cirrostratus clouds

Cumulus clouds

Clouds of all kinds

Clouds come in all sorts of shapes, sizes, and colors, from white, wispy "mares' tails" to towering, gray thunderclouds. English pharmacist Luke Howard devised a system of classifying clouds in 1803. He identified 10 distinct categories of clouds, all of which are variations on three basic cloud forms—puffy cumulus clouds, layered stratus clouds, and feathery cirrus clouds. This system is still used by meteorologists today.

Sheet clouds

Altostratus are high, thin sheets of clouds that can often completely cover the sky, making the sun look as if it is seen through misty glass.

Fleecy clouds

Altocumulus are medium-height, fluffy rolls of clouds with dark, shadowed sides.

Shower clouds
Bigger and darker than cumulus, cumulonimbus often bring thunderstorms and heavy rain.

Cloud spreads out at the top where the air stops rising at the tropopause (the top of the troposphere). This is sometimes called the "anvil," because it is shaped like an old blacksmith's anvil.

Temperature here –40°F (–40°C)

Violent updrafts and downdrafts in the front wall of clouds create hailstones

Temperature here 32°F (0°C)

Flying saucers
Lens-shaped lenticular clouds form over mountain ranges. They usually stay stationary.

Mainly ice crystals

Strong updrafts carry billows of clouds high into the atmosphere

Mixture of ice crystals and water

Mainly water droplets

Air drawn in here

Trailing virga

Cumulus clouds may let rain or ice crystals fall into drier, slower-moving layers of air. The streaks that result, known as "virga," evaporate before they reach the ground.

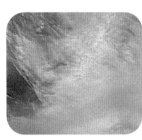

An icy veil

Cirrostratus occurs when cirrus spreads into a thin, milky sheet. Here, the sun appears very bright and may be surrounded by colored rings.

Fluffy clouds

Cirrocumulus are made of ice crystals and often form a pattern known as a "mackerel sky" as the clouds look like the scales of a mackerel.

A gray blanket

Stratus are vast, dull clouds that hang low over the ground and may give a damp drizzle. Higher up, they appear as fog.

Cumulus layer

Stratocumulus often form when the tops of cumulus clouds rise and spread out sideways into sheets. They look like a blanket of rolling clouds.

Mares' tails

Cirrus clouds, made entirely from ice crystals, form high in the sky, where strong winds blow the crystals into wispy "mares' tails."

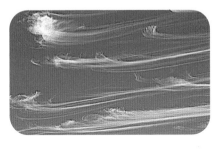

Cauliflower clouds

Cumulus clouds often mass together and grow upward, with dense, white heads like cauliflowers. If they keep on growing, they may become rain-bearing cumulonimbus.

A rainy day

Raining fish

Every year during the main rainy season in Yoro, Honduras, fish often rain from the sky right after a thunderstorm. It may be because waterspouts during the storms pick up the fish offshore and deposit them inshore as the storms decay, although this claim is disputed.

Dark, slate-gray clouds are a sure sign of rain. In the tropics, huge cumulonimbus clouds can tower 9 miles (15 km) into the sky, unleashing sudden torrential downpours. Lighter, thinner nimbostratus clouds provide slow, steady rain that may last for hours, or even days. Low stratus clouds give persistent drizzle that is little more than a mist.

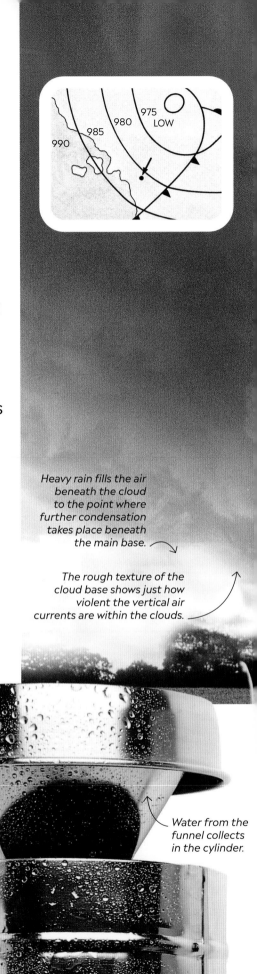

Heavy rain fills the air beneath the cloud to the point where further condensation takes place beneath the main base.

The rough texture of the cloud base shows just how violent the vertical air currents are within the clouds.

Water from the funnel collects in the cylinder.

Light or heavy

Rain is described as light if less than 0.09 in (2.5 mm) falls in an hour and heavy if more than 0.29 in (7.6 mm) falls. In the midlatitudes, heavy rain does not usually last long. Even the worst downpours are rarely heavier than those seen most days in many tropical areas.

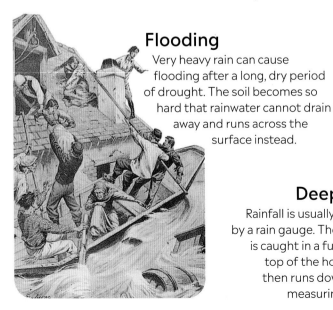

Flooding

Very heavy rain can cause flooding after a long, dry period of drought. The soil becomes so hard that rainwater cannot drain away and runs across the surface instead.

Deep water

Rainfall is usually measured by a rain gauge. The rainwater is caught in a funnel at the top of the hollow drum, then runs down into the measuring cylinder.

Cloudburst

A cumulonimbus cloud will start to die when its cold, downward air currents overwhelm its warm upcurrents. At this point, the cloud releases all its water at once in a cloudburst.

Rolls of clouds form as rain sweeps the colder air downward, forcing warm air upward to create another cloud.

Rain falling from the base of the cloud

Storm waters

Storms at sea can create huge waves that cause flooding in coastal regions.

Deluge

Some of the world's heaviest rain is brought by monsoon winds. In Cherrapunji in India, monsoon rains once brought 16 ft (4.8 m) of rain in 15 days.

Rain falling from clouds

Fronts and **lows**

In the midlatitudes—the areas between the tropics and the polar regions—much of the year's most unpleasant weather comes from great, spiraling weather systems called depressions, or lows. Depressions produce swirls of clouds that bring cloudy skies, blustery winds, rain, and even snow. A big depression may be a thousand miles wide, but it usually passes over in less than 24 hours.

Wisps of cirrus

Warm front

Veils of cirrostratus

Wispy warning
When long streaks of wispy cirrus clouds are seen high in the sky, they often signal a change of weather and the onset of a depression. Cirrus clouds form right at the top of a warm front (see below) and are made entirely of ice.

Wind here light and blowing away from the front

Cold polar air

A warm front

When a mass of warm, tropical air meets cold polar air, a boundary called a front develops between them. A warm front often signals the arrival of a depression. Here, the warm, moist tropical air slides up over a wedge of cold, polar air, producing clouds. As the front moves forward, cirrus clouds form at the edge, followed by a veil of cirrostratus clouds. Within a few hours, the clouds thicken at the base of the front, first with altostratus and then with nimbostratus. Rain—or even snow—starts to fall. The rain lasts for hours, before clearing up for a short break before the cold front arrives.

Wind here blowing strongly almost parallel to the front

Air masses

Wind and weather are linked by air masses—vast chunks of the atmosphere that are either wet or dry, or cold or warm throughout. Dry, cold air masses form over continents near the poles, while warm, moist ones form over tropical oceans. Weather largely depends on which air mass is overhead at the time. Far inland, a single air mass can stay in place for a long period, bringing stable weather. In coastal areas, a shift in wind direction can bring a different air mass and a weather change. The most changeable, stormy weather usually occurs along a front—the point at which two air masses meet.

Continued on next page

EACH TO ITS OWN

Each part of the world has its own type of air mass, bringing its own kind of weather. Warm, wet, tropical ocean air brings warm, humid weather, while cold, wet, polar ocean air can bring snow.

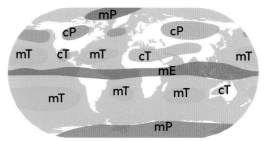

Polar continental (cP), Tropical maritime (mT), Polar maritime (mP), Tropical continental (cT), Equatorial maritime (mE)

Veiled warning
When the sun is faintly visible through a thin veil of altostratus, it is time to begin seeking shelter, as rain is not far away.

First rain
As the front approaches, the sky darkens and the first drops of rain may fall—even before the thick nimbostratus clouds arrive.

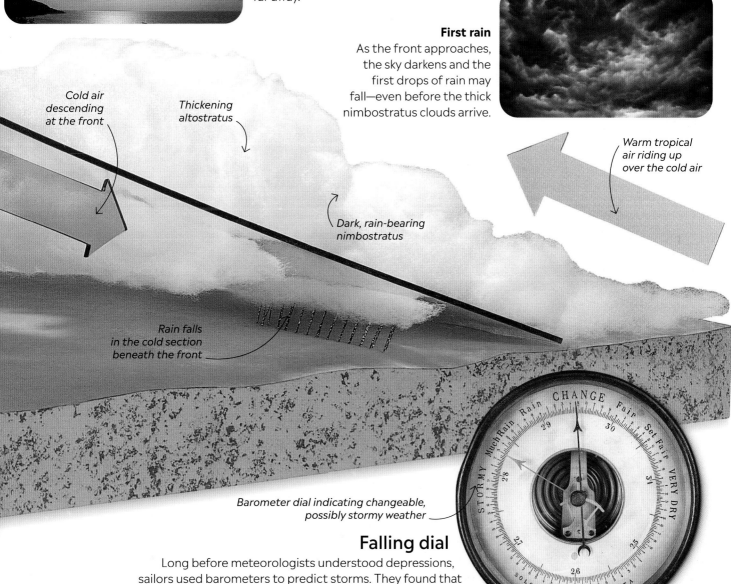

Cold air descending at the front

Thickening altostratus

Warm tropical air riding up over the cold air

Dark, rain-bearing nimbostratus

Rain falls in the cold section beneath the front

Barometer dial indicating changeable, possibly stormy weather

Falling dial
Long before meteorologists understood depressions, sailors used barometers to predict storms. They found that a rapid drop in air pressure was a sure sign of bad weather.

Continued from previous page

A cold front

After the warm front has passed, the weather becomes milder, and thick nimbostratus clouds give way to lighter stratocumulus. But the lull is short-lived. Thickening cumulus clouds warn of the coming cold front, where cold polar air cuts in sharply beneath the warm, moist tropical air. The cold front slopes more steeply than the warm front, and strong updrafts can stir up violent storms. Huge cumulonimbus may build up, bringing heavy rain or thunderstorms. But although the storms can be intense, they usually pass within an hour or so.

Storm warning

In the past, sailors were warned of storms by a coded system of cones, hoisted at coast guard stations.

High-level winds blow the icy tops of the clouds out in a sharp wedge

Huge cumulonimbus clouds

Rapidly rising warm air

Advancing cold front

Brewing storm

There is no mistaking the towering, gray cumulonimbus clouds that build up along a cold front.

Winds along the front are often strong and gusty

Heavy rain falls in various places all along the cold front

Squalls

Cold fronts often bring sudden, violent gusts of wind and rain known as squalls.

Sunset calm
As the front moves away to the east, the skies clear, leaving a few cumulus clouds toward the setting sun. High above, strong winds in the upper atmosphere create dramatic streaks of icy clouds across the sky.

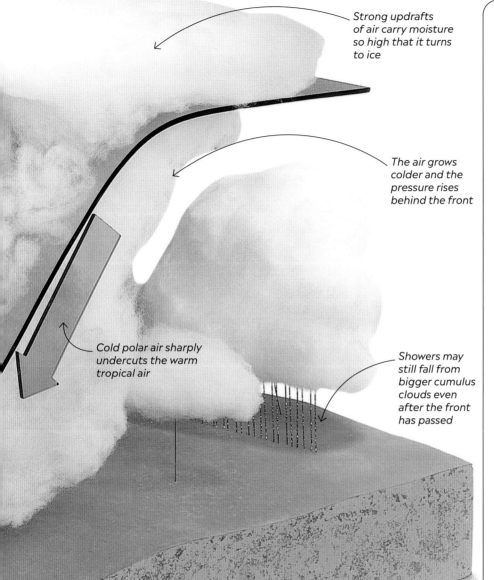

Strong updrafts of air carry moisture so high that it turns to ice

The air grows colder and the pressure rises behind the front

Cold polar air sharply undercuts the warm tropical air

Showers may still fall from bigger cumulus clouds even after the front has passed

Depression forming in the northern hemisphere

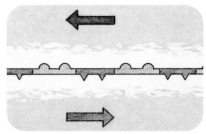

1. Depressions start when cold polar air and warm tropical air meet at the polar front.

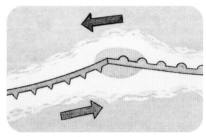

2. The two air masses rotate around an area of low pressure caused by rising warm air.

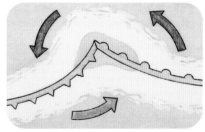

3. The kink in the polar front develops two arms—the warm front and the cold front.

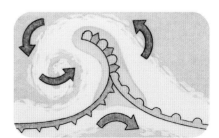

4. The cold air wraps around the depression, separating the warm air from the center of the storm.

DEPRESSIONS

Many depressions begin over the sea, where warm, moist, tropical air meets cold, dry, polar air along an imaginary line called the "polar front." An area of low pressure, or depression, forms when the warm tropical air bulges into the cold polar air. The cold air rushes in to replace the rising warm air, causing the winds to spiral.
If the upper atmosphere is favorable for cyclone development, the depression deepens and the polar front develops a definite kink.

Thunder and lightning

When a black, towering cumulonimbus cloud unleashes a deluge of thunder, lightning, wind, and rain, the effect can be awe-inspiring. Big thunderclouds can tower 10 miles (16 km) or more in the air and create enough energy to light a small town for a year. Cumulonimbus clouds are formed by strong, turbulent updrafts of warm, moist air. They are most common in the tropics, where massive storms often break in the afternoon, after the morning sun has stirred up the air.

Lightning

Thunderclouds are masses of air, water, and ice. Inside, violent air currents cause ice crystals to smash into each other, causing static electricity. Ice crystals at the base of the cloud are negatively charged, while the ground and the top of the cloud are positively charged. The great difference in electrical charges makes electricity leap between different parts of the cloud (sheet lightning) or between the cloud and the ground (fork lightning).

Strike!

Lightning tends to strike tall objects like trees, which is why it is dangerous to shelter under one in a storm.

Storm god

To ward off violent storms, priests in Nigeria prayed to the storm god Sango.

👁 EYEWITNESS

Controlling lightning

Scientists working on the European Laser Lightning Rod Project in Switzerland are developing a system to guide lightning away from certain areas using a powerful laser beam. This will help protect sites such as power plants and airports.

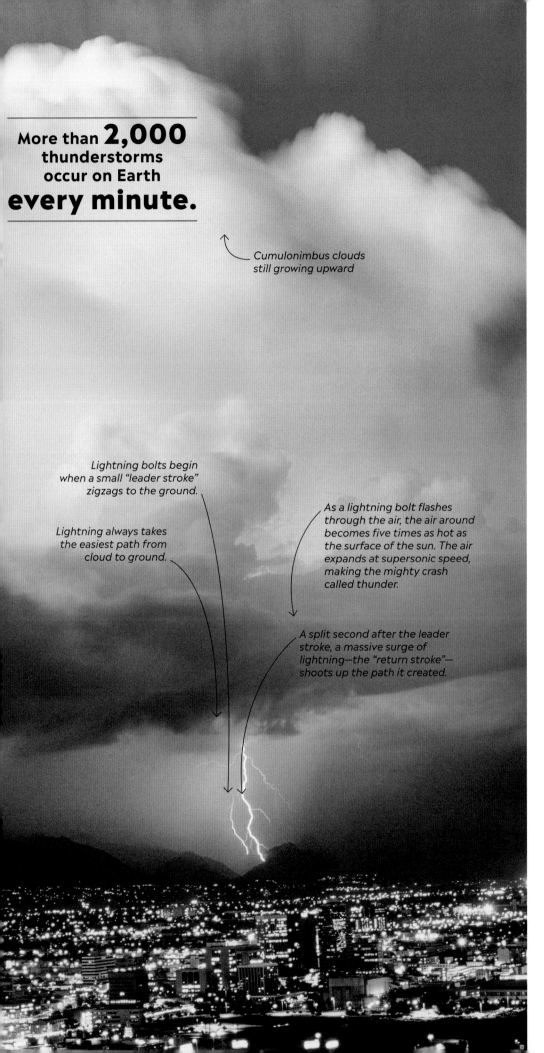

More than 2,000 thunderstorms occur on Earth every minute.

Cumulonimbus clouds still growing upward

Lightning bolts begin when a small "leader stroke" zigzags to the ground.

Lightning always takes the easiest path from cloud to ground.

As a lightning bolt flashes through the air, the air around becomes five times as hot as the surface of the sun. The air expands at supersonic speed, making the mighty crash called thunder.

A split second after the leader stroke, a massive surge of lightning—the "return stroke"—shoots up the path it created.

It's electric

In 1752, US inventor Benjamin Franklin carried out experiments with kites to prove that lightning was electricity.

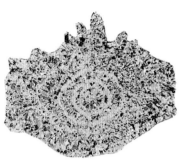

Hail and hearty

A section of one of the largest hailstones ever found, which weighed 1.7 lb (768 g), fell in Coffeyville, Kansas, in 1970. Special illumination shows that it is made of alternate layers of clear and opaque ice.

Having a ball

People have reported a strange phenomenon called ball lightning. In 1773, there were reports of a glowing ball in a fireplace that burst with a loud bang. These rare sightings have never been explained.

Monsoon

For six months of the year, most of India is parched and dry. But every May, the monsoon comes. A moist wind blows in from the Indian Ocean and the skies grow dark with clouds. For six months, torrential rain sweeps north over the country until the wind dies down and the rains slacken. By December, the land is dry once more. Similar rainy seasons occur in many other places in the tropics, such as northeast Australia and East Africa.

The monsoon can lash tropical coasts with intense rain, wind, thunder, and lightning.

The monsoon brings some of the world's most torrential rains.

Band of rain moving rapidly across open grassland

Torrential winter rain in Saigon, Vietnam

Heavy downpour

Between October and March each year, the northeast winter monsoon brings moisture from the South China Sea to Indonesia, Malaysia, Vietnam, and Thailand. Cool air picks up moisture and becomes unstable as it flows over the warm ocean surface, leading to intense rainfall and flooding.

MONSOON REGION

Monsoons affect large areas of the tropics, from the Caribbean to northeast Australia. Monsoons result in wet and dry seasons in the tropics.

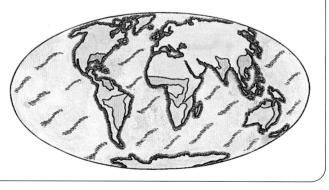

After the deluge

Monsoon rains can cause severe flooding. In India and Bangladesh, the low-lying delta of the Ganges River is particularly prone to floods.

High cumulonimbus clouds

Mountains force the monsoon upward, causing even more rain: Cherrapunji in the Assam mountains is one of the wettest places in the world.

Large cumulonimbus clouds pile up against high ground as the monsoon blows inland.

Some areas may stay dry and parched even while neighboring areas are being drenched.

Dragon's breath

The monsoon rains are vital for crops in most of Asia. In China, they were symbolized by the dragon, who brought the precious gift of water.

SOUTHWEST AND NORTHEAST MONSOONS

The hot, dry lands of Asia draw warm, moist air from the Indian Ocean in early summer.

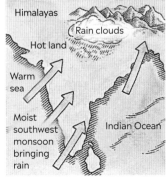

Himalayas
Rain clouds
Hot land
Warm sea
Moist southwest monsoon bringing rain
Indian Ocean

Southwest monsoon

The cold, dry winter air spreads out from central Asia, bringing chilly, dusty conditions.

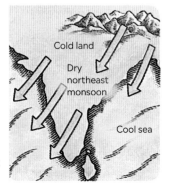

Cold land
Dry northeast monsoon
Cool sea

Northeast monsoon

A snowy **day**

Snow forms when tiny ice crystals in clouds stick together to form snowflakes. Outside the tropics, most rain starts off as snow, but it usually melts before it reaches the ground. Snow can occur at very low temperatures, but the heaviest snowfalls usually occur when the air temperature is closer to freezing, as warmer air can hold more moisture. In fact, more snow falls in a year in southern Canada and the northern US than at the North Pole.

Under very cold conditions snow remains loose and powdery and is often whipped up by the wind.

Fresh snow can contain as much as 90-95 percent air and protects the ground from much colder temperatures above the surface.

Snow rescue
Freshly fallen snow contains so much air that people can survive beneath it for a long time.

Snow flowing down the mountain as a glacier

Rivers of ice and air
Snow builds up on high ground where temperatures are low. It turns into ice, which slowly flows down valleys as glaciers. Cold, heavy air above the ice caps follows the same paths, bringing icy winds to the lowlands beneath.

👁 EYEWITNESS

The snowflake man
W. A. Bentley (1865–1931) was an American farmer and an expert in photomicrography—photography of tiny objects. He spent more than 40 years photographing snowflakes through a microscope. He called snowflakes "tiny miracles of beauty" and snow crystals "ice flowers."

Snowflakes
Snowflakes occur in a variety of shapes, and no two are identical. All natural snowflakes are made of ice crystals and have six sides.

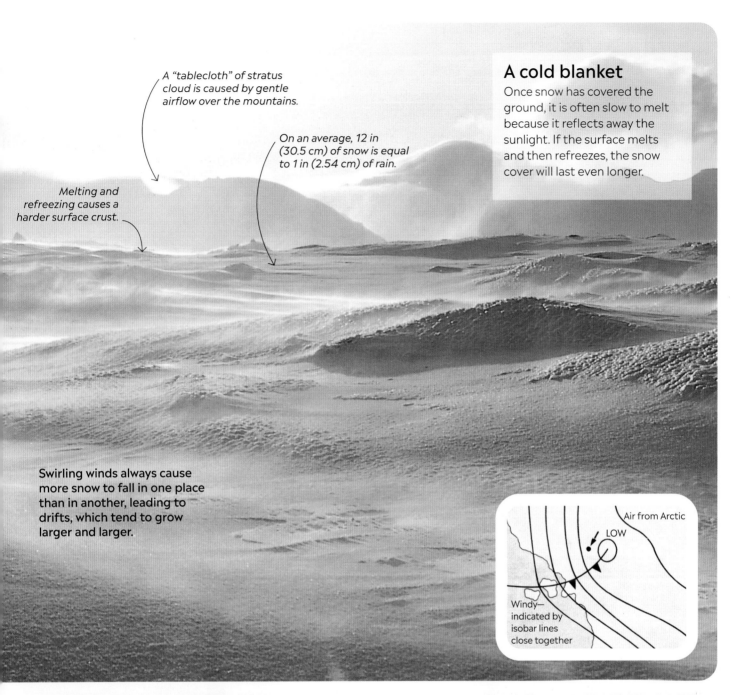

A "tablecloth" of stratus cloud is caused by gentle airflow over the mountains.

On an average, 12 in (30.5 cm) of snow is equal to 1 in (2.54 cm) of rain.

Melting and refreezing causes a harder surface crust.

A cold blanket
Once snow has covered the ground, it is often slow to melt because it reflects away the sunlight. If the surface melts and then refreezes, the snow cover will last even longer.

Swirling winds always cause more snow to fall in one place than in another, leading to drifts, which tend to grow larger and larger.

Air from Arctic

LOW

Windy— indicated by isobar lines close together

Avalanche
Avalanches happen when fresh, loose snow builds up on a harder, icy layer. The slightest disturbance can start a slide, which crashes downhill, burying everything in its path.

Snow covered
Sapporo, the snowiest city in the world, receives 235 in (597 cm) snowfall a year. This is due to its unique location, next to mountains and the Sea of Japan. Together, researchers from the University of Utah and Japan's Nagaoka Snow and Ice Research Center are studying these high-impact snowfalls.

Wind

Wind is the movement of air around Earth. Sometimes it moves slowly, giving a gentle breeze. At other times, it moves rapidly, creating gales or hurricanes. Gentle or fierce, wind always starts in the same way. As the sun moves through the sky, it heats up some parts of the sea and land more than others. The warm air above these hot spots becomes lighter than the surrounding air and begins to rise. Elsewhere, cool air sinks because it is heavier. Winds blow wherever there are differences in the temperature of the air.

Wind tower

In the 1st century BCE, the Greek astronomer Andronicus built an eight-sided Tower of Winds (above). Each face was carved with one of the eight wind spirits, one for each direction the wind blew.

Chinese fliers

The ancient Chinese were flying kites as long ago as 500 BCE. Some were shaped like dragons to frighten enemies. Others were shaped like socks to indicate the strength and direction of the wind—just like modern windsocks today.

Head points into the wind, indicating the direction the wind is blowing from

Catching the wind

Long, thin flags like this pennant were often flown on ships to show which way the wind was blowing. In the Middle Ages, similar colorful pennants would flutter over battlefields. Archers would use them to figure out the wind direction when aiming their bows.

Vane warning

Weather vanes swing around to show where the wind is blowing from. In Christian countries, vanes are often in the form of weathercocks (above). Weathercocks first adorned church roofs in the 9th century CE, as a reminder of the cock that crowed when St. Peter denied Christ three times.

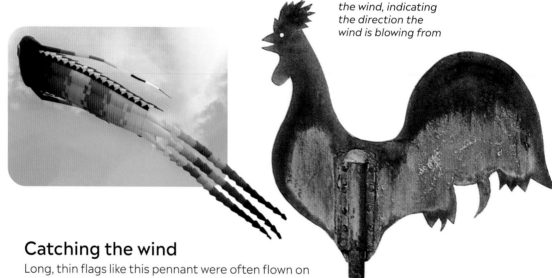

Cross indicating north, east, south, and west

Hoist rope

Wind instrument

This digital anemometer is used to measure wind speed, providing readings to a high level of accuracy. Able to be used both indoors and outdoors and during the day or the night, the instrument is far easier to operate than older, bulkier machines.

Wind speed reading

Modern digital anemometer

Cups spin around at high speed—just how fast depends on the strength of the wind

WORLD WINDS

The world's winds are part of a global system that moves air between the equator and the poles. At the poles, cold air sinks and moves toward the equator. At the equator, warm air rises and moves toward the poles. Because Earth is spinning, winds do not travel in straight lines. They bend to the right north of the equator and to the left in the south. This bending of the winds is called the Coriolis Effect.

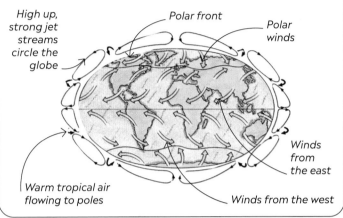

High up, strong jet streams circle the globe

Polar front

Polar winds

Winds from the east

Winds from the west

Warm tropical air flowing to poles

Wind scale

In 1805, the British admiral Sir Francis Beaufort devised a scale for measuring winds at sea by observing their effects on sailing ships and waves. Beaufort's scale was later adapted for use on land and is still used today. Wind strengths are based on a 13-point scale from Force 0 (calm) to Force 12 (hurricane).

Force 0 is complete calm.

Force 6 is a strong breeze, giving some large waves and "white horses" at sea.

Force 10 is a storm, causing high waves.

Rotors turn wind vane into the wind

Wind vane to show wind direction

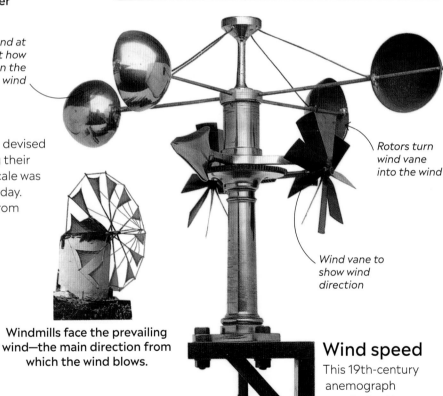

Windmills face the prevailing wind—the main direction from which the wind blows.

The average wind speed is recorded on graph paper as this cylinder rotates.

Wind speed

This 19th-century anemograph was devised to measure wind speed. The speed at which the cups rotate in the wind is continuously recorded as a cylindrical chart driven by clockwork.

Tropical storms

Also known as typhoons and tropical cyclones, hurricanes are the most violent and destructive storms on Earth. Winds can gust up to 250 mph (400 kph), and vast areas

Hurricane winds can damage or flatten buildings

are swamped by torrential rain. Hurricanes begin as small storms over warm, tropical oceans. If the sea temperature is above 80°F (27°C), several storms may cluster and swirl together, fed by strong winds in the atmosphere. Soon they drift westward across the ocean, drawing in warm, moist air and spinning in ever-tighter circles. At first the eye (center) of the storm may be more than 200 miles (300 km) across. As it moves west, it gains energy from the warm air it draws in. By the time it reaches the far side of the ocean, the eye has shrunk to 30 miles (50 km) across, and winds howl around it at hurricane force.

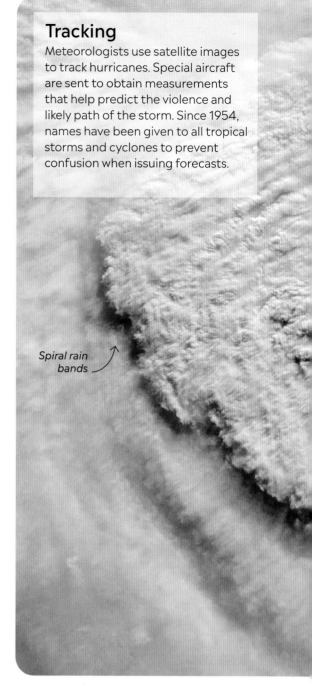

Tracking

Meteorologists use satellite images to track hurricanes. Special aircraft are sent to obtain measurements that help predict the violence and likely path of the storm. Since 1954, names have been given to all tropical storms and cyclones to prevent confusion when issuing forecasts.

Spiral rain bands

ANATOMY OF A HURRICANE

Hurricanes develop above warm ocean waters. Moist, rising air causes an area of very low pressure. Surrounding air spirals inward and forms curved clouds called rainbands. In intense storms, a calm, clear eye forms in the center. Surrounding the eye is the eyewall, a ring of deep thunderstorms accompanied by the storm's strongest winds.

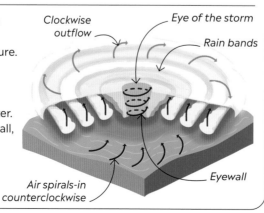

Clockwise outflow

Eye of the storm

Rain bands

Air spirals-in counterclockwise

Eyewall

Mixed blessing

Much of the vegetation on tropical islands depends on the torrential rain brought by hurricanes. But the raging winds can also destroy crops.

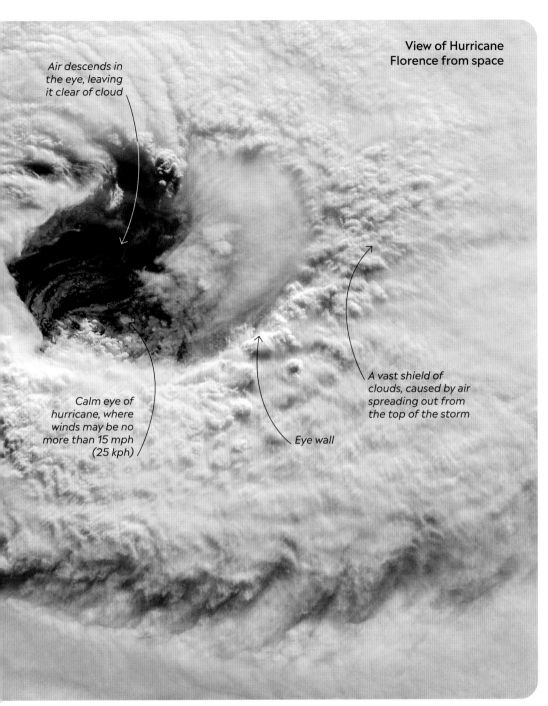

View of Hurricane Florence from space

Air descends in the eye, leaving it clear of cloud

A vast shield of clouds, caused by air spreading out from the top of the storm

Calm eye of hurricane, where winds may be no more than 15 mph (25 kph)

Eye wall

(1) Day 1: thunderstorms develop over the sea.

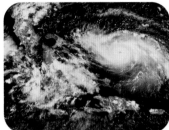

(2) Day 2: storms group to form a swirl of cloud.

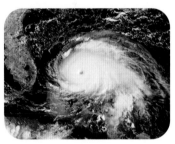

(3) Day 3: winds grow and a distinct center forms.

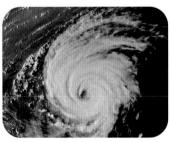

(4) Day 5: eye forms, hurricane is at its most dangerous.

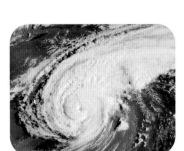

(5) Day 8: eye moves over land, after which hurricane subsides.

Atlantic hurricane

The satellite images show Hurricane Dorian over the Atlantic. First, warm air rises from the ocean forming cumulonimbus clouds and bands of thunderstorms (1). A swirl of clouds develops gradually (2). The winds become stronger and rotate around a single center (3). An eye develops, just inside the ring of the most destructive winds (4). When the storm passes over land, it loses its energy source, and the winds drop rapidly (5).

45

Whirling Winds

Tornadoes, also known as twisters and whirlwinds, are whirling spirals of wind that leave a trail of destruction wherever they strike. The deadly funnel of spinning air roars past in just a few minutes, sucking people, cars, and buildings high into the air, before smashing them to the ground. Tornadoes form inside giant storm clouds called supercells, and may strike wherever there are thunderstorms.

Waterspout
When a tornado occurs over the sea, it is called a waterspout. These often last longer than tornadoes but tend to be gentler, with wind speeds of less than 50 mph (80 kph).

Supercell cloud

Funnel touching down in a whirling spray of dust and debris

1. Swirling column
Tornadoes form within vast thunderclouds, where a column of rising warm air is set spinning by winds near the ground and at the top of the cloud blowing in different directions. They can rotate at speeds of up to 300 mph (482 kph).

2. Whirling devil
As the funnel touches the ground, the tremendous updraft in its center swirls dust, debris, cars, and people into the sky. Chunks of wood and other objects become deadly missiles as they are hurled through the air by the winds. A tornado reduces houses in its path to matchwood and rubble yet can leave those just a few yards outside its path untouched. Sometimes a tornado will whirl things high into the air then set them gently down, unharmed, hundreds of yards away.

Flying roofs

The strong winds of tornadoes can lift off the roofs of houses. When the roof is whisked away, the rest of the house disintegrates. Falling debris during a tornado can also damage a roof.

Dusty menace

Unlike tornadoes and waterspouts, which spin down from clouds, "dust devils" are formed in the desert by columns of hot air whirling up from the ground. Although less dangerous than their name suggests and weaker than tornadoes, they can still cause damage. Up to 1.2 miles (2 km) tall, they usually do not last more than a few minutes.

Funnel lifts away from the ground

3. Spinning funnels

For a moment, the funnel lifts away from the ground and the houses beneath are safe. But any second it may touch down again. This is a large tornado, and within it there is not just one spinning funnel but several, each revolving around the main one. The tornado dies down as it runs out of moist, warm air at the bottom or cool, dry air sinks from the cloud.

Mild spin

Tornadoes are especially violent in central US, but they can strike wherever thunderstorms occur, as shown in this engraving of a whirlwind in England.

47

Fog

Lighthouse
In very dense fog, sailors may not be able to see the warning lights of lighthouses and have to rely on foghorns and sirens.

When the wind is light, skies are clear, and the air is damp, moisture in the air can turn into water droplets near the ground, forming mist or fog. The fog clears when the sun comes up and begins to warm the air. Radiation fog is the most common type of fog. It forms when heat from the ground radiates (escapes) into space. The air above the ground cools and condenses into droplets, forming fog that spreads slowly upward. Fog also forms by advection, where a warm, moist wind blows over a cool surface.

Over the sea, temperature does not always fall far enough to form fog

Deadly fog
In 1956, the UK government passed the historic Clean Air Act, restricting use of coal. This was in response to a thick, toxic smog that had lasted for five days in London in 1952. Smoke from many coal fires had combined with fog and become trapped near the ground, polluting the air and killing up to 12,000 people.

Smog
Urban areas are prone to thick fog because they are often situated in low-lying areas close to water. When fog combines with smoke, it forms heavy, polluted air called smog. In some cities, cyclists wear masks to protect them from smog caused by cars and factories.

Light winds bring in new air to sustain mist

California fog

In San Francisco, California, the Golden Gate Bridge is often engulfed in thick advection fog that rolls in from the Pacific. It forms when warm, moist air from the south blows over cool ocean currents flowing from the Arctic. As it moves inland, the fog quickly evaporates as it moves over the warm surface of the land.

Fog is actually tiny droplets of water condensed from the air

Fog spreads slowly upward from the surface of the water

Two fogs

Some coastal fog is a mixture of both radiation and advection fog. On a warm day, a sea breeze may bring cool, moist air inland. At night, most of this drifts back to sea. Some sea air may linger and cool until it condenses to form fog.

Upside down

Fog forms just above the ground, or water, and spreads upward, but only so far. The air gets warmer around 1,640 ft (500 m) above the ground. This is called a temperature inversion, and fog does not rise above this point. Inversions are common in places like British Columbia, Canada (left).

49

8:30 a.m.
At the start of the day, the un is too cool to stir the air—which is why hot-air balloons are often launched at dawn.

11:20 a.m.
By midmorning, the early morning cumulus clouds are growing and have even produced a few showers.

2:15 p.m.
If the air is unstable enough, rising air currents within cumulus clouds may begin to form deeper cumulonimbus clouds with icy tops.

Early morning cumulus clouds

High cirrus clouds

Growing cumulus clouds

Tops of cloud beginning to turn to ice

Deep cumulus cloud

Dawn to dusk
This sequence shows the changing weather on a spring day in the midlatitudes.

A day of weather

Hot-air ballooning on a fine summer day

The weather can change dramatically during the course of a single day. In many tropical regions, fine, sunny mornings are followed by a massive buildup of thunderclouds as the sun stirs up strong updrafts of air. Usually this is followed by a brief downpour in the afternoon and a clear dusk. In the midlatitudes, changes in the weather are often caused by a depression, which can turn warm sunshine into icy rain in just a few hours.

3:00 p.m.
By midafternoon, clouds can build up so much that thunderstorms occur. Here, clusters of clouds have joined together. Storms and heavy rain are nearby.

3:45 p.m.
A huge, gray cumulonimbus cloud darkens the sky, its top hidden by lower clouds. Gusts of wind warn of torrential rain.

5:15 p.m.
The heavy clouds start to move away, although rain is still falling. Sunlight strikes through the cloud illuminating the raindrops and creating a rainbow.

Icy head of cloud spread out by high level winds

Rain

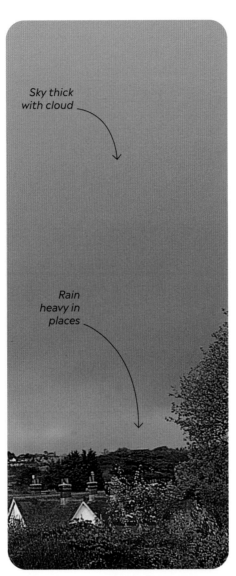

Sky thick with cloud

Rain heavy in places

Sky starting to lighten behind cloud

Rainbow

Castles in the air
If a layer of warm air forms over a cold sea, distorted images of distant objects can sometimes be seen in the water. They are created when the warm air bends light rays from images of objects that are normally invisible beyond the horizon.

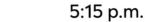
Cirrostratus   Altostratus   Cumulus

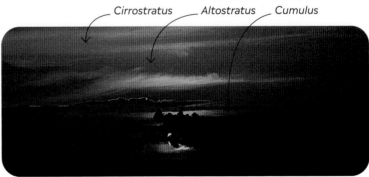

7:00 p.m.
By sunset, the wind has dropped and the band of showers has moved away, leaving a few scattered cumulus clouds. In contrast to the clear sky of the morning, middle-level clouds show that an area of low pressure is approaching from the west bringing unsettled weather.

Mountains

At the top of Mount Everest, winds howl at up to 192 mph (320 kph), and the temperature often drops as low as –94°F (–70°C). Even on lower mountains, winds tend to be much stronger than on the plains. Above a certain height—known as the snow line—many mountains are permanently coated in snow and ice. Because mountains reach so far into the atmosphere, they have an effect on wind and cloud patterns, forcing air to move up or down as it passes over their peaks.

At the top

Many weather stations are built on mountains, such as this observatory at the base camp of Mount Everest. In May 2019, a team of climate scientists and Sherpas (Indigenous Himalayan people) successfully installed a weather station only a few hundred yards from the mountain's summit— the highest in the world.

 EYEWITNESS

Low pressure

Blaise Pascal (1623-1662) was a French physicist and mathematician. In 1648, he proved that the atmosphere has its own weight, or pressure. He measured the air pressure at the top and bottom of a mountain and found that the pressure was lower at the top because there was less air weighing down on it from above.

Clouds and snow

In many mountain ranges, the highest peaks may reach above the clouds, basking in bright sunshine. However, the peaks are usually icy cold, since any heat from the sun is reflected straight back into the atmosphere by the snow. Near the equator, only the very highest peaks are permanently covered in snow as it is too cold here for rain. Toward the poles, however, the snow line is much lower.

Peaks stand clear of the clouds

Permanent snow cover

Wisps of icy cloud

At night, cold air may drain into the valleys, making them very cold

Wet peaks

Mountaintops tend to be wet and misty—especially if in a moist air stream. Pacific island mountains, like these in Tahiti (below), are among the dampest places in the world. Mount Wai-'ale-'ale in Hawaii is always surrounded by wet cloud and receives more than 457 in (11,600 mm) of rain each year.

Temperature drops by about 43°F (6°C) for every 3,280 ft (1,000 m) rise.

North-facing slopes are always in deep shadow and bitterly cold—so cold that ice breaks up the rocks making them steep and craggy

Air pushed up the mountain slopes often fills valleys with clouds

Alpines

Tiny flowers, called alpines, have managed to adapt to the cold, sunny weather of mountains such as the Alps in Europe.

High winds

Mountain tops are nearly always windier than open, low country. This is partly because wind strength increases with height, and partly because winds rush over, rather than around, mountain peaks.

Air warms and dries as it descends over the leeward side

Leeward side

Air lift

When warm, moist air moves toward a mountain range, it is forced upward. As it rises, it cools and condenses to form heavy rain-bearing clouds that make the slope on the windward side very wet. As the air passes over the mountains, it warms and loses its moisture, leaving the leeward (downwind) side of the mountain much drier. This is known as the rain shadow effect.

Rain at the summit

Rising air cools and condenses into clouds

Moist air is forced upward by mountain range

Windward side

On the plains

Winter hunters
Millions of buffalo once roamed the North American grasslands, providing food for local Native American tribes. The hunters wore snow shoes to stop their feet from sinking into the snow.

Far from the sea, the world's vast, flat plains tend to have hot summers and dry, cold winters. Rain falls mostly in the summer when the strong sun stirs up heavy showers and thunderstorms. In winter, rainfall is rare, although fall snowstorms may deposit a covering that lasts until spring. In the shadow of mountain ranges, many plains are so dry that only scrub, or grass, can grow.

The driest state in the US, Nevada receives only 9.5 in (24 cm) of rainfall each year on average.

Parched lands
Most of the world's deserts are plains, such as North America's Nevada (left). Air over the desert warms as it descends, creating dry conditions. It then moves outward, preventing moist air from entering the plain.

Mega storms
In 2018, around 150 scientists from countries including Argentina, the US, and Brazil joined together to study the severe thunderstorms in central Argentina, to the east of the Andes mountains. Their research showed that although the storms were powerful, conditions were unfavorable for tornadoes. These results improved weather warnings.

Extreme weather
Clear, dry skies over the plains can lead to extreme variations in temperature. Winters are bitter, with temperatures well below freezing. In summer, the hot temperatures of the day drop sharply once the sun goes down.

Wave clouds
Mountain ranges often disturb winds blowing across them, forming waves of cloud that hover for hours in the upper atmosphere.

Skies are often clear, giving hot summers and cold winters

Smooth, lenticular clouds often form in bands on the leeward side of mountain ranges, building up like piles of plates.

With little to slow them down, the dry winds can be very strong in the plains.

Low rainfall leads to scrubby, stunted vegetation.

LOW

HIGH

Sizzling summers

Summer on the plains can be extremely hot. On July 10, 1913, temperatures in Death Valley, California (above), reached 134°F (56.7°C).

Dust to dust

In the 1930s, the American Midwest suffered a serious drought. Strong winds blew clouds of thick, choking dust from the ground, forcing many families to leave their farms.

Coastal areas

The presence of so much water gives weather by the sea its own particular characteristics. Coastal areas tend to be wetter and cloudier than inland areas. Cumulus clouds, for instance, usually form inland only during the day, but on coasts facing the wind, they drift overhead at night as well. Sea fogs, known as advection fogs, can linger for days and are caused by warm air blowing over cool water. The weather in coastal areas is generally less extreme than further inland. Because the sea loses heat slowly, nights tend to be warmer on the coast, with milder winters and slightly cooler summers. Frosts are rare on sea coasts in the midlatitudes.

Frequent, salt-laden winds blowing from the sea dry the exposed sides of trees and shrubs, killing leaves and buds so the plants look as though they are leaning away from the wind.

LOW

Blown away

Seaside resorts can often be quite windy, as illustrated in this 20th-century postcard. This is partly because there are no obstacles across the open sea to stop the winds from blowing hard, and partly because temperature differences between land and sea often create stiff breezes.

Clear coast

This picture shows the coast of Oregon in the northwest US, but it is typical of west coasts everywhere in the midlatitudes. Deep depressions are common at this latitude, and here, a cold front has just passed over and is moving inland. Cloud lingers in the upper air, and cumulus clouds are still forming, signaling that further showers are on the way. As the front moves inland, it may well produce increasingly less rain since there is less moisture in the air inland.

Coastal fog

As water in the oceans is slow to heat up, sea fog tends to linger until the wind changes direction. Off the coast of Newfoundland, Canada (left), where warm westerly winds blow over cool currents from the Arctic, thick fogs can last for days.

Lingering clouds from cold front

Visibility tends to be good on coasts, partly because winds are stronger, but mainly because the air is much cleaner over the sea.

Growing cumulus clouds

Waves begin to break in shallow water, where the water is less than twice as deep as the wave.

Lack of "white horses" on the waves shows the wind is only light

Wind and waves

Even when the weather is locally calm along the coast, large waves can be generated by strong winds thousands of miles away, within distant storm systems such as tropical cyclones or midlatitude depressions. This phenomenon is known as a swell and can help windsurfers by creating large, breaking waves along the coast.

Warmer air from over the sea is drawn over the land to replace the cool air that is sinking

Air rising over the warm sea pushes air at high altitude toward land

Land cools quickly

Nighttime land breeze

Sea cools slowly

Sinking air over the land drives air seaward on the surface, creating a land breeze

Air pushed out to sea at high altitude increases the air pressure over the cool sea

Air sinks over the cool sea

Sinking air over the sea and rising air over the land drive sea air shoreward, creating a stiff sea breeze

Air rises over the warm land about 0.6 mile (1 km) above the ground

Land and sea

Coasts are often quite windy, with sea breezes in the daytime and land breezes at night. During the day, the land heats faster than the sea, and air begins to rise. As the warm air rises, cool air from the sea is drawn in below, creating a stiff sea breeze. At night, the land cools more quickly, and air begins to sink. The cool air pushes out under the warm air over the sea, creating a land breeze.

Land warms up quickly in the sun

Sea warms up slowly

Daytime sea breeze

Colors in the sky

These images are in fact the enlarged shadows of mountain climbers on clouds.

Pure sunlight is white, but it is made up of the seven colors of the rainbow mixed together. As sunlight passes through the atmosphere, the colors are scattered in different directions by gases, dust, ice crystals, and water droplets. Sometimes, sunlight strikes ice and water in the air to create spectacular effects such as rainbows. These colorful arcs form in showery weather and always appear on the opposite side of the sky to the sun. Occasionally, electrical discharges can bring vivid color to the sky, particularly at night.

Water colors

Rainbows are sunlight that is bent and reflected by raindrops. As the light passes through a raindrop, it bends slightly. It is reflected from the back of the drop and bent again as it leaves the front. The different colors bend at different angles, which makes them separate. Red always appears at the top of the rainbow, followed by orange, yellow, green, blue, indigo, and violet.

Rainbow is created by reflection from rain in a cloud much higher in the sky

Saintly light

In thundery weather, sailors might see a strange, glowing ball of light on the masthead. Called "St. Elmo's Fire," this is actually an electrical discharge, like lightning.

Rainbow god

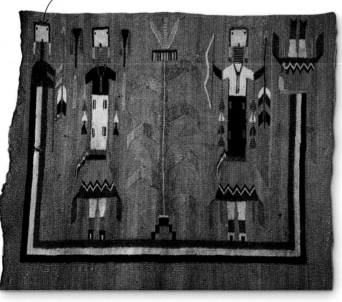

Rainbow spirit

The Navajo people of southwest US regard the rainbow as a spirit. The spirit is depicted on this blanket around two other supernatural beings, with a sacred corn plant in the center.

More than one sun

A colorful halo, or ring around the sun is caused by ice crystals in the clouds bending sunlight. They sometimes also create bright spots, called sun dogs, that look almost like other suns.

From airplanes, a rainbow can sometimes be seen as a full circle.

Receding cumulonimbus cloud

Red on the top, or outside, of a "primary" rainbow

Yellow in the rainbow's center

Low, stratus-type clouds in shadow

Violet on the bottom, or inside, of the rainbow

Polar lights

Occasionally, electrically charged particles from the sun strike gases in the atmosphere high above the poles to create a spectacular display of colored lights in the night sky. These lights are called auroras.

Moonbow

On rare occasions, raindrops catch the reflection of bright moonlight to form a moonbow. The colors of the moonbow are the same as those seen in a rainbow.

Climate change

Since Earth's atmosphere formed around 4 billion years ago, its climate has gone through many changes. One of the most dramatic changes occurred 10,000 years ago, during the last Ice Age. The weather became so cold that a third of the Earth's surface was covered in ice more than 790 ft (240 m) thick. Now, scientists are unanimous that human activity is warming the atmosphere, endangering our very existence.

Viking voyage

Between 1000 and 1200 CE, the world's weather became so warm that much of the Arctic ice cap melted. At that time, Viking voyagers were sailing across the Atlantic, settling in Iceland and Greenland, and even reaching America. But between 1450–1850, during the little Ice Age, the cold weather returned, destroying Viking communities.

Preserved in ice

Ice from glaciers shows what the climate was like during the Ice Age. Bubbles of air in the ice reveal that the atmosphere contained fewer of the gases that cause global warming.

Meteor

It is thought that the dinosaurs became extinct about 66 million years ago, when a huge meteor struck Earth, sending up so much dust that the sun's rays were blocked out, making the planet very cold.

Growing evidence

Each ring in a tree trunk shows one year's growth. If rings are wide apart, the weather was warm; if close together, then the weather was cold.

Climate in crisis

Meteorologists believe that the world is getting warmer due to increased greenhouse gases in the atmosphere. Greenhouse gases trap heat and keep Earth warm, like the panes of glass in a greenhouse. But increasing human activity—such as burning fuels to power factories and vehicles—has pumped more of these gases into the atmosphere, making Earth too warm. Carbon dioxide is the main greenhouse gas, but harmful chemicals from aerosol sprays and refrigerators also contribute to the greenhouse effect. If Earth becomes just a few degrees warmer, some places will become largely uninhabitable, endangering human life.

Melting ice

Global average sea level rises since the 1990s have mostly been caused by the melting of glaciers and the Greenland Ice Sheet, alongside ocean warming.

Hole in the sky

Ozone is a bluish gas high in the atmosphere that helps protect us from the sun's harmful ultraviolet rays. Recently, a hole has appeared in the ozone layer over the Antarctic – shown in this satellite photograph—and ozone levels have declined. The chemicals causing the damage are being phased out and ozone levels have begun to recover.

The death of the forest

Every year, tropical forests equivalent to the size of Iceland are cut and burned to make temporary cattle pasture. Forests are made largely from carbon. If they are cleared and burned without being replaced, the carbon is released into the air as carbon dioxide—one of the main greenhouse gases that contribute to global warming.

Global warming

Scientists agree that on average, the world will warm between 2.7 and 7.2°F (1.5 and 4°C) by the year 2100, unless we take far-reaching and drastic action now. The Intergovernmental Panel on Climate Change (IPCC) reports show that temperature rise will vary with different levels of emission. The IPCC says that cuts in emissions, especially of carbon dioxide, can control temperature rise significantly.

IPCC chairman Hoesung Lee at the World Climate Summit, 2018

Home weather station

Professional meteorologists have a great deal of sophisticated equipment and thousands of weather stations to help them track the weather. But you can easily keep your own weather watch using simple instruments at home. The main thing is that you take your readings at exactly the same time at least once every day. The most important readings are rainfall, temperature, wind speed and direction, and air pressure, but you could also record cloud cover, soil temperature, and humidity.

Weather stations
Modern wireless weather stations allow you to analyze and display your data by connecting to a computer or directly to the internet. Although expensive, they allow you to view your data from anywhere in the world.

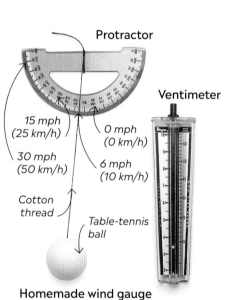

Protractor

Ventimeter

15 mph (25 km/h)

0 mph (0 km/h)

30 mph (50 km/h)

6 mph (10 km/h)

Cotton thread

Table-tennis ball

Homemade wind gauge

Wind speed
You can make a wind gauge using a table-tennis ball tied to the center of a protractor. Hold the protractor parallel to the wind so the ball is blown sideways. By reading the angle of the thread on the protractor, you can estimate the strength of the wind. A ventimeter (above) is much more accurate but more expensive.

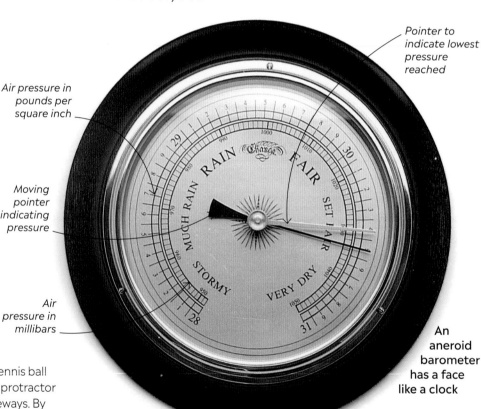

Pointer to indicate lowest pressure reached

Air pressure in pounds per square inch

Moving pointer indicating pressure

Air pressure in millibars

An aneroid barometer has a face like a clock

Air pressure
Barometers are expensive, but if you have one at home, you can use it to predict the weather. A drop in air pressure indicates storms, while a rise in pressure signals good weather.

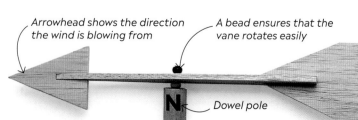

Arrowhead shows the direction the wind is blowing from

A bead ensures that the vane rotates easily

N

Dowel pole

Wind direction
You can make a wind vane from balsa wood and a dowel pole. Make sure the vane's head is smaller than its tail and use a compass to figure out exactly where north and south are.

Soil

Special, right-angled thermometers (above) are used to measure soil temperature.

Cloud snaps

Photographs provide a visual record of weather conditions. Make a note of the exact time and date when the photo was taken. Drawing clouds is also a good way of learning to tell one type from another.

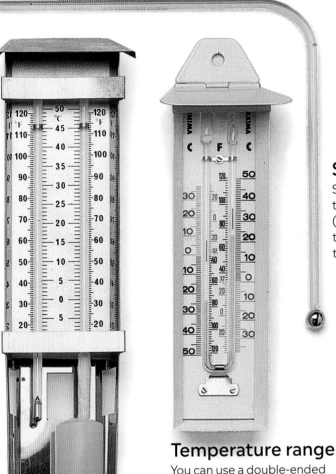

Humidity

A wet and dry hygrometer (above) has two thermometers: one bulb is wet, the other dry. The difference in temperature between them indicates the level of humidity.

Temperature range

You can use a double-ended thermometer (above) to record the maximum and minimum temperatures reached each day. A magnet is used to reset the indicators every time a reading is taken. Make sure the thermometer is not in direct sunlight.

Screens

Professional weather instruments are kept inside ventilated shelters (left) to protect them from direct sunlight.

Measuring cylinder

Rain gauge

Rainfall

A plastic rain gauge is quite accurate, as long as you set it up securely at ground level in an exposed place. Take out the measuring cylinder each day to make a reading. Remember to empty it and dry it thoroughly.

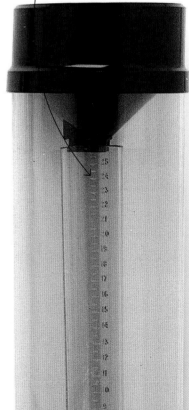

Readings

Keep a record of all instrument readings, with the date and time. Readings must be taken at the same time each day, even in heavy rain.

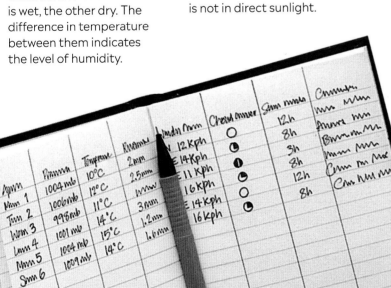

Did you know?

AMAZING FACTS

In very cold winters, waterfalls sometimes freeze over. Ice grows out from the side of a waterfall as splashed drops of water freeze, one on top of the other.

Frozen waterfall in the Zanskar Range, Himalaya mountains, India

The atmosphere contains 1.5 billion cubic miles (2.4 billion cubic km) of air and about 34 trillion gallons (15,470 trillion liters) of water. Because of gravity, 80 percent of the air and nearly all the moisture are in the troposphere, the part of the atmosphere closest to Earth.

Sunbathing can be dangerous even on cloudy days. The clouds reflect so much ultraviolet light from the sun that they increase the amount of harmful rays that reach the ground, increasing the risk of skin cancer.

Very hot weather can kill. If it is too hot or humid for people's sweat to evaporate and cool them down, they get heatstroke. This can lead to collapse, coma, or even death.

The biggest desert in the world is Antarctica. It has only about 5 in (127 mm) of precipitation (snow or rain) a year, just a little more than the Sahara Desert.

It can snow in the desert. In winter, snow sometimes falls in cold deserts, such as the Great Basin in the US and the Gobi in Asia.

In 1939, hundreds of frogs fell from the sky during a storm in England. They had probably been sucked up from ponds and rivers by small tornadoes then dropped to the ground again with the rain.

A staggering 110 million gallons (500 million liters) of rain can fall from a single thunderstorm.

Raining frog

Many reported sightings of UFOs have turned out to be lenticular clouds. Waves of wind around mountain tops form rounded clouds like flying saucers that hover motionless for hours.

Hailstones sometimes grow enormous. The largest known hailstone in the world

Lenticular cloud

fell on Vivian, South Dakota, in 2010 and had a diameter of 8 in (20 cm). The heaviest one on record (2.25 lb/1 kg) fell on Bangladesh in 1986.

Trees in forests around the world are being destroyed by acid rain. Acid rain forms when pollutants from factories and cars react with sunlight and water vapor in the clouds to form sulfuric and nitric acids. These contaminate water supplies and damage forests and crops.

The average cloud lasts for only about 10 minutes.

Conifers destroyed by acid rain

QUESTIONS AND ANSWERS

Why does the weather keep changing all the time?

Heat from the sun keeps the air in motion. The sun's power to heat the air varies, depending on its height in the sky. These variations cause the weather to change constantly.

What makes the wind blow?

Winds occur wherever there are differences in air temperature and pressure. They blow from areas of high pressure to areas of low pressure.

Solar corona

Why are there sometimes colored rings around the sun?

A solar corona appears when the sun is covered by a layer of cloud. Water droplets in the cloud split the sunlight, creating a rainbow effect.

What makes a large, bright disc around the moon?

A lunar corona occurs when sunlight reflected from the moon passes through water droplets in cloud.

How has the weather made desert rocks such strange shapes?

Over time, rocks are worn away by weather. Temperature changes and water make rocks crack and shatter. Also, windblown sand wears away softer rock, leaving strange shapes, such as pillars and arches.

Why are some deserts hot in the day and freezing at night?

Above hot deserts, the skies are clear. The ground becomes baking hot by day as there are no clouds to shield it from the sun, but it turns cold at night because there is nothing to trap the heat rising up into the atmosphere.

How big do the biggest clouds grow?

The biggest clouds are cumulonimbus, the big, dark rain clouds that produce thunderstorms. They can be up to 13 miles (21 km) high and hold half a million tons of water.

What is a mirage and where do they appear?

Mirages are tricks of the light created by very hot air. Air close to the ground is much hotter than the air above it, and light bends as it passes from one temperature to the other. This creates a shimmering reflection that looks like water. Deserts are renowned for producing mirages that look like oases.

How powerful is the average thunderstorm?

A typical thunderstorm, about 0.6 miles (1 km) across, has about the same amount of energy as 10 atomic bombs.

Earth pillars in Alberta, Canada

When is the best time to see a rainbow?

The best rainbows often appear in the morning or late afternoon, when the sun is out and rain is falling in the distance. Stand with your back to the sun and look toward the rain to see the rainbow.

RECORD BREAKERS

⚡ **The coldest place:**
The lowest temperature recorded in the world is –128.6°F (–89.2°C) at Vostok Station, Antarctica, on July 21, 1983.

⚡ **The hottest place:**
At Death Valley, California, the temperature reached a record high of 134°F (56.7°C) on July 10, 1913.

⚡ **The driest place:**
María Elena South in Chile's Atacama Desert is the driest recorded place on Earth, with a relative humidity in the soil as low as that on Mars.

⚡ **The wettest place:**
Mawsynram in India is the wettest place in the world, receiving an average annual rainfall of 467 in (1,187 cm).

Desert mirage

Weather power

Pollution from human activity is changing the climate. To reduce the amount of pollutants in the atmosphere, scientists are using the power of the weather to provide alternative, cleaner sources of energy.

The WC-130 normally carries a crew of six people and is equipped with data-gathering instruments.

GENERAL WEATHER WEBSITES

- Weather Underground provides live weather data: **www.wunderground.com**
- The UK Met Office's award-winning website is at: **www.metoffice.gov.uk**
- Australia's Bureau of Meteorology site: **www.bom.gov.au**

Hurricane Hunters

A US Air Force squadron, known as the Hurricane Hunters, flies aircraft through hurricanes to monitor them and predict when and where they will hit land. The specially adapted aircraft pass through the eye (center) of the hurricane every two hours and send back information on the hurricane's intensity and movement to the National Hurricane Center.

Research scientists studying ice in Antarctica

Antarctic research

In Antarctica, meteorologists carry out experiments to make long-term predictions about climate change. Other scientists study climate changes in the past and the effects of current global warming. Oceanographers and biologists research the changing ocean conditions in the icy seas around Antarctica and their effects on plant and animal life.

Life in the freezer

Meteorologists based at research stations in Antarctica carry out detailed research into changing climate conditions. They also monitor the hole in the ozone layer that lies above Antarctica to find out how pollution and our efforts to prevent it are affecting the atmosphere.

TORNADO ALLEY

In the US, tornadoes regularly affect the eastern half of the country, with the highest risk regions in Tornado Alley (South Dakota to Texas, plus Missouri) and in the southeast (Mississippi and Alabama).

**US Air Force
WC-130
aircraft**

FIND OUT MORE

- Find out about hurricane hunters at: **www.hurricanehunters.com**
- For information on storm chases, visit: **www.stormchase.com**
- Discover more about the research in Antarctica at: **www.usap.gov**
- Find out about alternative technology at: **www.cat.org.uk**
- Alternatively, you could visit a specialized center to see working examples of wind, water, and solar power in action and to learn more about alternative energy sources.

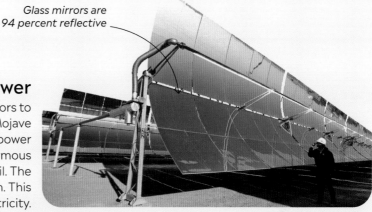

Glass mirrors are 94 percent reflective

Solar power

Solar power stations use thousands of wide mirrors to gather the energy from sunlight. Luz, in the Mojave Desert, in California, has one of the biggest solar power stations in the world. A series of 170,000 enormous solar mirrors reflect heat onto tubes filled with oil. The hot oil heats water, which in turn makes steam. This drives turbines that generate electricity.

Tidal power

Energy from the tides can be converted into electricity by building a barrage across an estuary (where a river meets the sea). As the water flows in and out, it passes through machines called turbines, which generate electricity. The biggest tidal energy plant in the world crosses the La Rance estuary in France. Local weather can affect tides.

La Rance tidal barrage, France

 E Y E W I T N E S S

Chasing storms

Storm chasers, like US engineer Tim Samaras (1957–2013), often risk their lives researching tornadoes using special radar equipment. Samaras, seen here with his special camera, studied tornadoes for over two decades, even designing his own weather instruments.

Blades are attached to a central hub

Catching the wind

At wind farms, windmills convert the wind's energy into electricity. Wind farms work only in exposed places, and it takes about 3,000 windmills to generate as much power as a coal power station.

Wind farm near Palm Springs, California

Floods at Fenton, Missouri (above)

Flood victims (above) wait to be airlifted from rooftops near Chokwe, Mozambique.

Extreme weather

Weather can be violent and cause extensive damage. Every year, devastating floods, savage storms, and long periods of drought occur across the world, causing increasing concern about climate change.

Hurricanes

Cyclone Nargis caused devastation when it struck Myanmar in May 2008. More than 90,000 people died, and around 55,000 were estimated missing. It was the deadliest natural disaster recorded in Myanmar.

Floods

Floods cause more damage than any other natural phenomenon. They swamp vast areas of dry land, destroying crops and making thousands of people homeless. In February 2000, Mozambique suffered its worst floods for 50 years, and more than a million people lost their homes.

The Dust Bowl

In the 1930s, the American Midwest had no rain for five years, and thousands of acres of land were turned into a desert known as the Dust Bowl. Hot winds caused suffocating dust storms, and about 5,000 people died from heatstroke and breathing problems.

Volcanic weather

Large volcanic eruptions affect global weather. When Mount St. Helens erupted in 1980, the entire top of the mountain blew off. Ash from the volcano was carried by high winds right around the planet, leading to hazy skies, amazing sunsets, and a brief drop in temperature.

The eruption of Mount St. Helens

Avalanches

When heavy snow builds up on a steep slope, even a small vibration can set off an avalanche. In Austria, in 1999, a block of snow weighing 187,000 tons crashed down on the village of Galtür, killing more than 30 people.

Rescuers using poles to search for victims of the Austrian avalanche

Avalanche on Mount McKinley, Alaska

Mudslides at La Guaira, Venezuela

Wildfire

Raging forest fires often start when lightning strikes vegetation during a long, dry period. On June 5, 2020, a lightning strike caused a forest fire in Arizona. It burned 119,978 acres (48,553 hectares) of land before it was finally put out on July 23, 2020.

Mudslides

In December 1999, 10,000 people were killed in Venezuela by devastating floods and huge mudslides. Torrential rain soaked into the hillsides creating fast-moving rivers of mud and debris, which destroyed all buildings, roads, and trees in their path.

69

Glossary

AIR MASS
A large body of air covering much of a continent or ocean, in which the temperature, pressure, and humidity are fairly constant.

AIR PRESSURE
The force of air pressing down on the ground or any other horizontal surface. Also known as atmospheric pressure.

ANEMOMETER
An instrument for measuring wind speed.

ANTICYCLONE
Also known as a "high," this is a body of air in which the air pressure is higher than it is in the surrounding air.

ATMOSPHERE
The layer of gases surrounding Earth, stretching about 600 miles (1,000 km) into space.

AURORA
Bands of colored light in the night sky. In the northern hemisphere, these are called the northern lights (*aurora borealis*); in the southern hemisphere, they are called the southern lights (*aurora australis*).

Anemometer

Barograph

BAROGRAPH
An instrument that provides a continuous record of air pressure on a strip of paper wound around a revolving drum.

BAROMETER
An instrument for measuring air pressure.

BLIZZARD
A wind storm in which snow is blown into the air by very strong winds.

CIRRUS
Feathery cloud that forms at high altitudes, where the air is very cold.

CLIMATE
The normal pattern of weather in a particular place or region, averaged over a long period of time.

CLOUDS
Masses of condensed water vapor and ice particles. There are three basic cloud forms: cumulus, stratus, and cirrus.

COLD FRONT
The boundary line between warm and cold air masses, with the cold air moving toward the area of warm air in front of it.

CONDENSATION
The change from a gas, such as water vapor, to a liquid, such as water.

CORIOLIS EFFECT
The effect caused by Earth's spin, which makes winds and currents follow a curved path across the planet's surface.

CUMULONIMBUS
A cloud that produces heavy showers and thunderstorms.

CUMULUS
A large, fluffy cloud with a flat base and rounded top.

CYCLONE
A body of air in which the air pressure is lower than it is in the surrounding air. Also known as a "low."

DEPRESSION
A weather system with a center of low pressure. It usually brings bad weather.

DEW
Moisture in the air that has condensed on objects at or near Earth's surface.

DEW POINT
The temperature at which water vapor in the air will condense.

DRIZZLE
Light rain made of drops that are smaller than 0.02 in (0.5 mm) across.

FOG
Water that has condensed from water vapor into tiny droplets near the ground, reducing visibility to less than 1,100 yd (1,000 m).

FRONT
The boundary between two air masses.

FROST
White ice crystals that form on cold surfaces when moisture in the air freezes.

GALE
A strong wind that blows at 32–63 mph (52–102 km/h).

GLOBAL WARMING
A long-term increase in the atmosphere's temperature, probably caused by the greenhouse effect.

GREENHOUSE EFFECT
The warming up of Earth's surface, caused by heat from the sun being trapped by gases in the lower atmosphere.

HAIL
Pellets of ice that fall from clouds.

Hygrometer

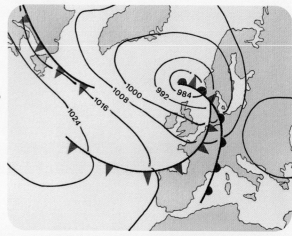

Weather chart showing fronts and isobars

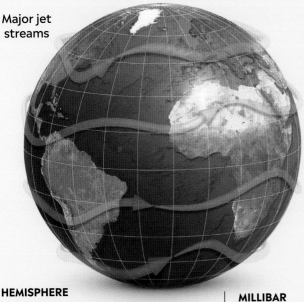

Major jet streams

JET STREAM
A band of very strong winds in the upper atmosphere.

LIGHTNING
A discharge of static electricity from a cloud. Sheet lightning occurs within a cloud. Fork lightning occurs between a cloud and the ground.

METEOROLOGY
The scientific study of weather.

commonly a haze that forms in polluted air in strong sunshine.

SNOW
Ice crystals that fall from clouds and stick together to form snowflakes.

STORM
Strong winds, between gale and hurricane force, of 64–75 mph (103–121 km/h).

STRATOSPHERE
The layer of Earth's atmosphere above the troposphere.

STRATUS
A vast, dull type of low-level cloud that forms in layers.

HEMISPHERE
Half of Earth. There are northern and southern hemispheres.

HOAR FROST
Spikes of frost that form when the air is about 32°F (0°C) and water vapor touches the surfaces of trees.

HUMIDITY
The amount of water vapor in the air.

HURRICANE
A tropical cyclone that occurs in the Caribbean and North Atlantic with winds over 75 mph (121 km/h).

HYGROMETER
An instrument used for measuring humidity.

ISOBAR
A line on a weather map that joins places with the same air pressure.

MILLIBAR
The unit used to measure atmospheric pressure.

MONSOON
A wind that brings alternate wet and dry seasons to India and Southeast Asia.

OZONE LAYER
A thin layer of ozone gas in the upper atmosphere that filters out harmful ultraviolet rays from the sun.

PRECIPITATION
All forms of water that fall to the ground or form on or near it, such as rain, snow, dew, and fog.

PREVAILING WIND
The main direction from which the wind blows in a certain place.

RADIOSONDE
A package of instruments attached to a weather balloon that sends data back to Earth.

RAIN GAUGE
An instrument used to collect and measure rainfall.

RAIN SHADOW
An area of lower rainfall on the lee (sheltered) side of a hill or mountain.

SMOG
Originally fog mixed with smoke, but now more

Sunshine recorder

SYNOPTIC CHART
A weather chart that gives detailed information about conditions over a large area.

THERMAL
A rising current of warm air.

THERMOSPHERE
The top layer of the atmosphere, above about 56 miles (90 km).

THUNDER
The sound made by expanding air during a flash of lightning.

TORNADO
A narrow spiral of air rotating at high speed around an area of extremely low air pressure. Wind speeds may be higher than 200 mph (320 km/h).

TROPOSPHERE
The lowest or innermost layer of Earth's atmosphere, where most of the weather takes place.

TYPHOON
A tropical cyclone that occurs over the Pacific Ocean.

WARM FRONT
A boundary line between two air masses where the air behind the front is warmer than the air ahead of it.

WATERSPOUT
A column of rapidly spiraling air that forms over warm and usually shallow water, or when a tornado crosses water.

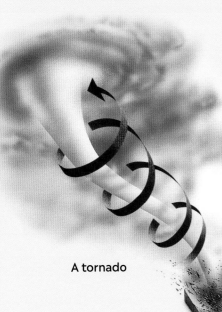

A tornado

Index

Acknowledgments

The publisher would like to thank the following people for their help with making the book:
Robert Baldwin of the National Maritime Museum, Greenwich, for making instruments available for photography; The Meteorological Office, Bracknell, for providing instruments for photography; Met Check for the loan of instruments on pp.62-63; David Donkin for weather models on pp.26, 34-33, 34-35, 44-45, and 53; Sophie Mitchell for her help in the initial stages of the book; Lisa Burke for assisting with revisions; David Ball, Neville Graham, Rose Horridge, Joanne Little, and Sue Nicholson for the wall chart; BCP, Marianne Petrou, and Owen Peyton Jones for checking the digitized files; Charvi Arora for editorial help; Hazel Beynon for text editing; Vijay Kandwal for DTP assistance; Saloni Singh and Priyanka Sharma-Saddi for the jacket; and Joanna Penning for proofreading and the index.

The publisher would like to thank the following for their kind permission to reproduce their images:

(Key: a-above; b-below; c-center; f-far; l-left; r-right; t-top; m=middle)

Alamy Stock Photo: Pictorial Press Ltd 6br, NASA Archive 13cra, RKive 13clb, Justin Kase zsixz 14cl, NASA Image Collection 15tl, Simon Maycock 15tr, The Picture Art Collection 16clb, Chris Cole 19, Tim Gainey 23cl, Design Pics 25bl, DPA picture alliance 36bc, Daniel J. Rao 38br, Vasa 38cl, David J. Green 43cla, Susan E. Degginger 44-45t, NOAA / Planetpix 45crb, NASA / UPI 45tr, 45cra, 45cr, Newscom 45bc, AC NewsPhoto 45br, Cultura Creative Ltd 46cl, 46cr, Michael Wheatley 49bc, Mark Green 52cl, Science History Images 52bc, Nick Albi 54bc, Daniel Kaesler 66bc, Izzet Noyan Yilmaz 66cl, ZUMA Press, Inc. 67bl, Phil Degginger 68-69b. **Alison Anholt-White:** 28cbr, 42cr. **Aviation Picture Library:** 20cl. **Bridgeman Art Library:** 17t,

17cr. **British Antarctic Survey:** 60c. **Bruce Coleman Picture Library:** 9cl, 14cr, 20c, 28br, 29bl, 52br, 54br, 54-55. **Corbis:** Bettmann 68tl; Gary Braasch 69tl; John H. Clark 66-67t; Philip James Corwin 67br; Graham Neden; Ecoscene 66crb; Jim Richardson 68bl; Kevin Schafer 67cra. **B. Cosgrove:** 24-25, 24tr, 25tl, 24tl, 25tr, 25tc, 28cl, 28clb, 29tr, 29ctr, 29cr, 29crb, 29br. **Dorling Kindersley:** Simon Mumford 17tr. **Dreamstime. com:** Manfredxy 2br, Omers 2cra, Gyuszko 18bl, Passigatti 21bl, 23tr, Thongchai Fueangluksnakul 30cl, Barna Tanko 30tl (Second image), Dleindec 33cr, Thomas Gowanlock 36cb, Mikle15 41bl, Lesuhova 42c, Dench 57tr, Platongkoh 58br, Alexander Shalamov 59bl, Andreas Bergman 61tr, Wirestock 62tr, Kanpisut Chaichalor 63tr, Shaun Miguel Perfectti 64tr, Wissanustock 65cla. **Dr. E. K. Degginger:** 7cbl, 13cbl, 34cl, 34bl, 35tr, 50cl, 50c, 50cr, 51tc, 51tl, 51br. **Planet Earth:** 18cr, 20br, 23bl, 41t, 53tr, 54clb, 55bl, 56b. **Popperfoto:** Peter Andrews/ Reuters 68cla; Andy Mettler/Reuters 69ca; Kimberly White/Reuters 69crb. **Ann Ronan Picture Library:** 6tl, 13cla, 14tl, 27bl, 27br, 38ca. **Royal Meteorological Society:** 28bl. David Sands: 25cl. **M. Saunders:** 20-21t Scala: 11ca. **Science Photo Library:** NASA EARTH OBSERVATORY / NOAA / NESDIS 7tr, HEATH MCDONALD 9tc, PATRICK DUMAS / EURELIOS 13b, British Crown Copyright, The Met Office 26br, KEITH KENT 36-37c, 40cb, 40crb, 40bc, Roger Hill 47c, Mike Hollingshead 58-59tr, 61cr, Simon Fraser 64cl, 64br; Damien Lovegrove 65bl; David Nunuk 65tr. **Shutterstock.com:** Alpha Pictures Entmt 28-29. **Stock Boston:** 48bc. **Tony Stone Picture Library:** 31t, 48-49, 52-53. **Wildlife Matters:** 8tr, 8tl. **Zefa:** 7cb, 7b, 24bl, 39t, 47tr, 50bl.

Dr. E. K. Degginger: 47cla. **E. T. Archive:** 12cb, 21br. **European Space Agency:** 12ca. **Mary Evans Picture Library:** 10bc, 20tl, 24br, 30bl, 44ca, 46tr, 53cr, 60cl. **Courtesy of FAAM:** BAE Systems Regional Aircraft 12-13t; With thanks to Maureen Smith and the Met Office UK. Photo by Doug Anderson 13cla. **Werner Forman Archive:** 18cl, 36bl, 39bl, 58bc, 60tr. **Courtesy of Kate Fox:** 22b. **Hulton Deutsch Collection:** 55bl. **Hutchison Library:** 31bl, 61clb. **Image Bank/ Getty Images:** Win McNamee 8br, Orlando SIERRA / AFP 30tl, Chuchart Duangdaw 41br, 43cb, Peter King 48bl, 56-57, Wolfgang Kaehler 60-61b, Simon Dawson / Bloomberg 61cla, STR / AFP 68c. **IPCC:** FAQ 12.1, Figure 1 (Chapter 12) from Collins, M., R. Knutti, J. Arblaster, J.-L. Dufresne, T. Fichefet, P. Friedlingstein, X. Gao, W.J. Gutowski, T. Johns, G. Krinner, M. Shongwe, C. Tebaldi, A.J. Weaver and M. Wehner, 2013: Long-term Climate Change: Projections, Commitments and Irreversibility. In: Climate Change 2013: The Physical Science Basis. Contribution of Working Group I to the Fifth Assessment Report of the Intergovernmental Panel on Climate Change [Stocker, T.F., D. Qin, G.-K. Plattner, M. Tignor, S.K. Allen, J. Boschung, A. Nauels, Y. Xia, V. Bex and P.M. Midgley (eds.)].

Cambridge University Press, Cambridge, United Kingdom and New York, NY, USA, pp. 1029-1136, doi:10.1017 / CBO9781107415324.024. 61br. **Istituto e Museo di Storia della Scienza (photos Franca Principe):** 2bl, 10bl, 10r, 11tl, 11crb, 11r, 11b. **Landscape Only:** 23cr. **Frank Lane Picture Library:** 20bl, 22tl. **Mansell Collection:** 18tl, 43cbl, 43cl. **Meteorological Office:** 12bl, 12br © Crown, 21t, 34t, 42tr, 49bl. **NASA:** SDO 16tl. **NASA's Earth Observatory:** Joshua Stevens 1c, 6cl; **National Centre for Atmospheric Research:** 37cra. N.H.P.A.: 44br. **R.K.Pilsbury:** 8crt, 8crb, 26-27, 32cl, 33cla, 34cl,

Illustrations: Eugene Fleury, John Woodcock

All other images © Dorling Kindersley
For further information see:
www.dkimages.com